Petra Kölle

300 Questions
About the
Aquarium

➤ Concise Information from A to Z
➤ Practical Tips from the Experts

BARRON'S

Contents

Anatomy and Behavior ?

Contents

■ Fish and Their Communities ❓

Feeding, Maintenance, and Water Quality ?

Contents

Recognizing and Treating Diseases ?

Appendix

Selection and Legal Issues

An aquarium gives you a fascinating glimpse of life under water. This chapter offers some interesting information about fish keeping and answers questions about legal issues as well as about selecting and buying fish and equipment.

Selection and Legal Issues

1. **Allergies:** Our daughter is very allergic to animal hair. She would like a pet, though, and we thought of an aquarium. Can fish trigger allergies, too?

   Aquarium fish are ideal pets for someone who is allergic to animal hair or feathers. However, many people are allergic to proteins found in bloodworms. These larvae are ingredients in many kinds of dry fish foods. If you are allergic to bloodworms, you should handle the flakes with tweezers and be careful not to get your face too close to the food container so that you do not inhale any allergenic particles.

2. **Animal Welfare Legislation:** Are fish protected under the animal welfare laws?

   In Germany, the Animal Welfare Law protects vertebrates, which includes fish along with amphibians, reptiles, birds, and mammals. It does not cover invertebrates (insects, spiders, snails, protozoa, and so on.) In the United States, however, the comparable Animal Welfare Act does not cover fish and other cold-blooded vertebrates.

EXTRA TIP

Outdoors in the summer
If you put in a small garden pond, you can use it from spring until fall to keep certain fish like Zebra Danios, Striped Panchax, Paradise Fish, White Cloud Mountain Minnows, or Goldfish. Put the fish in the pond on a warm day when the water temperature is at least 64°F (18°C). If you do this exactly as you would when adding new fish to an aquarium, the fish will not be harmed by the move. In fact, if you live in the southern United States, many species can be kept outside permanently.

The German Animal Welfare Law states, among other things, that you must keep an animal in a manner appropriate for its species and you may not cause an animal prolonged or repetitive pain or suffering. As an aquarist, you are thus legally obligated as well as morally obligated to inflict no harm on your fish. This means you must first find out about the specific requirements of your fish in order to give them the best-possible care. According to the German Animal Welfare Law, you are also not permitted to kill an animal without "reasonable grounds." One example of reasonable grounds for fish is an incurable disease. On the other hand, getting rid of a fish when it has grown too big for your aquarium or is too aggressive toward the other fish is not reasonable grounds. Similarly, if your efforts at breeding have produced too many baby fish, you cannot just kill them. Regardless of the legal status of your fish, as a responsible aquarist, you should find out how big a fish gets before you buy it and think about what you will do with any surplus fish.

3. **Breeding: Are our ornamental fish actually bred here, or are they imported from their country of origin?**

The majority of the fish on the market come from breeders in Southeast Asia. Ornamental fish are also bred on a large scale in North and South America as well as in Africa, Israel, and the Czech Republic.

Only an insignificant number of ornamental fish are bred in captivity in northern latitudes because the costs for captive breeding are very high. These are primarily species kept only by aquarium specialists or a few fish hobbyists and for which there is a correspondingly small demand. For example, captive breeding of many species of egg-laying toothcarps in commercial hatcheries would not be profitable.

4. **Buying Fish: I would like to buy my first fish. Are there some basic guidelines that I should follow?**

?

If you would like to buy fish, the first thing you should do is learn as much as you can about the requirements of the species you are considering. Then pay attention to the following guidelines when buying your fish:

➤ Wait until after you have set up your aquarium and allowed it to cycle for a few weeks before buying any fish.

➤ Do not go shopping when the store is busiest. Go on a weekday morning when there will not be as many customers.

➤ Take your time, and look around the store carefully.

➤ Are all the tanks clean? Do the fish as well as the plants appear healthy? Do not buy any fish that looks sick.

Live-bearing Guppies are very popular aquarium fish.

➤ Are sick fish in the display tanks? That is not a good sign. A responsible dealer will keep ailing fish in a quarantine tank or declare an infected tank off limits.

➤ Never buy stock from a tank in which there are dead fish, because you will risk introducing disease into your tank.

➤ Do not buy any fish from tanks with discolored water, because they are being treated with medications.

➤ Ask the dealer questions, and let him or her help you make your selection. A good pet dealer or breeder will take the time to give you detailed advice.

➤ After your fish have been properly packaged for transport, take them home as quickly as possible.

5. **Buying Fish: Is it better to buy juvenile fish or full-grown ones?**

You generally do not have the opportunity to choose between adults and juveniles of a species. Many species, for example Angelfish, are almost always sold as juveniles. The longer it takes to rear these fish, the more it costs, so they are usually sold as soon as

EXTRA TIP

Buying fish
Before you go shopping, make a list of the fish you would like to buy and learn as much as you can about them from specialized literature. What are their requirements? What sort of tank are they suitable for? Are the fish compatible? The best place to buy your fish is from a pet dealer, especially one who will guarantee the stock. Here you will usually receive expert advice and find fish that have gone through quarantine and are already acclimated.

possible, i.e., while they are still young. Species like Guppies and Swordtails, on the other hand, are sold almost exclusively as adults because they do not display their splendid coloration until the onset of sexual maturity.

You can usually enjoy juveniles for a longer time, they are generally less expensive, and you can watch them grow and develop. As a rule, young fish acclimate more easily to the water conditions in a new tank, but they are usually more sensitive than fully grown fish. However, the juveniles of many species do not display the beautiful colors of adults. In addition, you can never predict how a young fish will develop, while you can tell immediately if a full-grown fish has any defects such as inferior coloration.

6. **Captive Bred Fish: How can I tell if a fish is captive bred or wild caught?**

You can not tell by looking at a fish if it was caught in the wild or bred in captivity—unless, of course, the captive bred fish have changes in their coloration or finnage resulting from selective breeding. As a general rule, all special varieties, for instance, fish with veiltails, are captive bred. The aquarist has been at work here and has selectively bred very specific fin shapes or unusual colors. Such animals would have no chance of surviving in the wild because of their conspicuous appearance. You can assume that popular species like Guppies, Swordtails, Angelfish, Zebra Danios, or Starlight Bristlenose Catfish are captive bred. If you are unsure about the origins of any of your fish, consult an expert, such as the local aquarium store owner. He or she should be able to answer your questions.

7. **Conservation:** During a vacation in Malaysia, I saw Asian Bonytongues in display tanks. Can I keep these fish at home?

Typically no, because this species is listed in Appendix I of the Convention on International Trade in Endangered Species of Wild Fauna and Flora (CITES). Appendix I animals may be kept only under certain conditions, for instance if they are captive bred and the breeder has the appropriate license to sell them. CITES regulates trade in endangered species. Depending on the degree of endangerment, animals are listed in Appendix I, II, or III. At present (status as of 2007), nine species of fish are listed in Appendix I of CITES; this means that they are strictly protected. For the good of all hobby participants, as well as of the protected fish species themselves, you should adhere strictly to all CITES guidelines.

INFO

CITES documents

For animals listed in Appendix I, you need CITES documents, which you get at the time of purchase. All CITES animals must be registered with the U.S. Fish and Wildlife Service if they have been imported into the United States, and they must be marked to prevent fraud. Captive-bred animals may have to be reported and registered with conservation authorities at the state or local level and thus may not be traded. Appendix I includes 68 species of fish. They require import and export permits to be traded. Most of these fish are marine species. Among the freshwater fish species, the Asian Bonytongue or Arowana (*Scleropages formosus*) is listed in Appendix I of CITES, while all sturgeon species are in Appendix II. You may have to register protected fish with your state or local conservation agency and present a certificate of origin.

8. **Discolored Water:** The water in some of my pet dealer's tanks is discolored. What does that mean?

If the water in individual tanks has a blue, green, yellow, or sometimes even a reddish color, this means that the pet dealer has added medications to treat the fish for a disease. Never buy fish from tanks like these, or you will run the risk of getting a sick fish. A serious dealer will not sell you any fish from a tank that is being medicated.

9. **Economic Importance:** How many ornamental fish are kept in aquariums, and what is the economic importance of the fish-keeping hobby?

The following estimates are based on 1.9–3 million aquariums in Germany, where 4–6 percent of German households have an aquarium. In addition, there are another 1.2 million garden ponds with ornamental fish. Altogether, approximately 80 million ornamental fish are kept in Germany.

According to data from the German pet industry's trade association, aquarium owners spend more for supplies than any other group of pet owners. In 2003, Germans spent $246 million on aquarium supplies, compared with $157 million for dog accessories and $189 million for cat accessories. From January to September 2003, according to Germany's Federal Statistics Office, $24 million worth of ornamental fish were imported into Germany. When you consider that these fish still have to pass through the hands of wholesalers and pet dealers, all of whom have to make a profit, you can assume that annual sales of ornamental fish in Germany amount to over $100 million.

10. **Fish Shows: Is it true that there are shows for aquarium fish like the ones for pedigreed dogs and cats?**

Yes; for example, there are shows for Discus, Koi, and fancy Guppies. Each association has drawn up standards for the different varieties, and judges use them to select the "best" fish at these shows. At Guppy competitions, for example, body shape, dorsal and caudal fins, and swimming behavior of the fish are evaluated. For Koi, judges rate the many different color varieties; the colors should be as pronounced as possible and clearly set off from each other. Body shape is also evaluated. Discus shows are similar. The more closely a fish corresponds to the standard, the more likely it is to win the title of champion.

11. **Furniture Style: We would like to redecorate our living room. Is it possible to have our aquarium match the new decor?**

The aquarium itself is usually made of glass or, more infrequently, of Plexiglas. The design of the aquarium stand and hood determine the style. Perhaps you can find a stand that goes with your new decor. The pet store should offer a large selection of hoods and stands in different designs. If you still cannot find anything that you like or that goes with the style of your new furniture, you can certainly hire a cabinet-maker to help you out. Just be sure that the hood has enough room for the required number of fluorescent bulbs. The higher your tank, the more fluorescent bulbs you will need. Choose a stand that is tall enough for you to watch the fish comfortably while you are sitting down. Naturally, it should be sturdy enough to bear the weight of the aquarium without difficulty.

12. Health: **How can I tell if the fish offered for sale are, in fact, healthy?**

Take your time observing the fish in your dealer's tanks. Check to see if they look normal and their behavior is typical for the species. The table "Recognizing Healthy Fish" will help with this. Changes in appearance or behavior are often an indication of disease. If you have even the slightest doubt about the health of a fish, do not buy it.

If you see sick or even dead fish among the apparently healthy fish in a tank, you can assume that disease-causing organisms are present there. Do not buy any fish from tanks like this.

13. History: **Which species of ornamental fish were the first to be kept in aquariums?**

Goldfish have been kept as pets in China since the 12th century A.D. At first, raising these fish was a privilege reserved for the emperor and other nobles, who selectively bred different varieties and kept them in valuable porcelain bowls.

It is not known precisely when the first Goldfish were introduced to Europe. However, they were bred for the first time in Holland in 1728. From 1870 onward, they were regularly bred in Germany as well.

Goldfish are cold-water fish. They have been kept in aquariums since the 19th century.

RECOGNIZING HEALTHY FISH

Swimming behavior	➤ Their movements are coordinated. ➤ They swim away if you approach them with the net. ➤ They stay in the water level typical for their species. ➤ Their swimming behavior is typical for their species (e.g., schooling fish swim in a group).
Body surface	➤ Their scales are unbroken, smooth, and shiny. ➤ There are no patches or reddish blotches indicative of disease. ➤ There is no excessive production of slime.
Body shape	➤ The appearance of the body is typical for the species. ➤ The fish is not emaciated nor does it have a distended belly or injuries. ➤ The head appears neither too large nor too small in proportion to the body.
Fins	➤ They are intact, not ragged. ➤ They are not damaged.
Color	➤ The coloration is intense and typical for the species. ➤ Important: The colors may appear washed out due to stress (e.g., during transport in the plastic bag).
Eyes	➤ They are clear and of equal size. ➤ They do not protrude excessively.
Feeding	➤ When offered food, the fish snap at it immediately.

The first tropical fish to become popular with aquarists was the Paradise Fish (*Macropodus opercularis*). It was introduced to Germany in 1876.

Incidentally, the glass aquarium, which makes it possible to observe fish not just from above but from the side as well, is a European invention. It appeared around 1850.

14. History: **How did fish keeping develop into a hobby?**

The actual father of fish keeping was Emil Adolf Rossmässler. In 1856, he published an article entitled "The Sea in Glass" in the German magazine *Die Gartenlaube*; this awakened the interest of a broad public in the emerging hobby of fish keeping. In the 19th century, because of technical limitations, in particular the lack of suitable equipment for heating the water, the first aquarium inhabitants were cold-water fish (e.g., Goldfish). Once fish keepers succeeded in developing equipment like electrical heaters, keeping tropical fish and even breeding them in captivity became relatively easy.

15. Importing: **Many of the fish sold in pet stores are imported from abroad. How are they transported?**

Most ornamental fish arrive by airplane. In order to survive the long journey, they must be well packaged in bags that are filled one-third of the way with water and two-thirds with air or oxygen. Air is used for labyrinth fish and callichthyid armored catfish since they breathe atmospheric air and cannot tolerate pure oxygen. In general, pure oxygen is used for all other fish species. The plastic bags are closed with rubber bands and packed in well-insulated Styrofoam boxes to keep the water temperature from dropping too much. This way fish can survive a trip halfway around the world without harm.

Naturally, this assumes that not too many fish are in the bag, because otherwise the water quality would deteriorate rapidly. Ornamental fish exporters usually let the fish fast for a few days before transport to prevent excessive fouling of the water with waste products. In many cases, anesthetics are also added to the bags. This slows the metabolism of the fish and thus reduces oxygen consumption. It also makes the fish calmer during transport.

16. Importing: **Is there any problem with buying a fish after it has traveled such a long distance?**

In general, imported fish go first to a wholesaler. A serious importer will watch the fish closely during the quarantine period and if necessary treat them

Float the closed plastic bag with the new fish on the surface of the water for a while. 1

After an hour, open the bag and add aquarium water. This will get the fish used to the new water quality. 2

before they are sold. Normally a fish that has been too stressed by transport is not offered for sale. To be on the safe side, you should always quarantine any new fish you buy. This gives you the best protection against introducing pathogens into your aquarium.

17. Information Sources: Where can I obtain information about the fish that I would like to keep in my aquarium?

There are many good guides and specialized books on aquarium fish as well as on individual species or families. If you are looking for the latest information on fish keeping, you should subscribe to a magazine about the subject. You can also find information on the Internet, even if some of the advice you find there is not always sound. Another good source of information for all areas of fish keeping is the local aquarium club. You'll usually find help for your problems here because there are always a few "old hands" who can give you valuable tips. Occasionally, night schools or private individuals organize seminars on aquarium topics as well. You can find useful addresses and suggested literature in the appendix of this handbook.

18. Introducing Fish: What is the correct way to introduce newly purchased fish to an aquarium?

The pet store will package your fish in special plastic bags for the trip home. If you are stocking a new aquarium, then be sure you have finished setting up your aquarium and allowed it to cycle for several weeks. If, however, you are buying fish to add to your old stock, you should first put them into a quarantine tank.

Here is how to release the fish from their carrying bag. First float the closed plastic bag on the water surface for a while so that the temperature in the bag can equalize with that of the aquarium water. After about thirty minutes to an hour, you can open the bag and add a little water from your aquarium. Repeat this every ten minutes for about one to two hours. The greater the difference between the water parameters of the dealer's tank and your aquarium, the longer this equalization process should take (see the photos on page 21). Most fish will not tolerate sudden changes in individual water parameters. Be sure to ask your pet dealer about the water parameters in the store's tanks and compare them with those of your tank.

19. Liability Insurance: We have a small 15-gallon (60L) tank. Is it a good idea to take out liability insurance?

As the owner of the aquarium, you are liable for all damage caused by your aquarium, whether in your own home or in a rented apartment. If your aquarium leaks and the ceiling of the apartment below you is damaged, you are responsible for that as well. Since even a relatively new tank can leak, you should take out liability insurance that expressly covers these damages, regardless of the size of your tank.

The attractively colored Clown Loach can get to be 12 inches (30 cm) long and therefore is suitable for only larger aquariums.

20. **Location: I would like to get an aquarium. What must I take into consideration when deciding where to put it?**

?

First of all, you would certainly want to set up your aquarium so that it fits in with your furnishings and gives you a good view of your fish. Apart from these aesthetic criteria, you should take into consideration a few additional guidelines when choosing the right location.

➤ First you must check to see whether the floor of your apartment or house is able to bear the weight of an aquarium. In a 125-gallon (500 L) aquarium, the water alone weighs about 1,000 pounds (500 kg). Add to this the weight of the decorations, the tank itself, and the stand. With larger tanks, the load-bearing capacity of the floor can quickly be exceeded.

This is less of a concern with new construction than old houses, for example those having a wooden beam floor. For large, heavy tanks, you should choose a spot next to a load-bearing wall to avoid overloading the floor.

➤ Make sure that your aquarium is not in a high-traffic area. If the fish are frequently disturbed by people going to and fro, the fish will be stressed. They can perceive the slightest vibrations and will then try to escape or hide.

➤ Placing the aquarium near an electrical outlet is very practical. Electrical cords trailing across the room are unsightly, and people can trip over them.

➤ To care for the fish and perform routine maintenance more easily, be sure that the tank and equipment are easily accessible.

➤ The floor covering around the aquarium should not be harmed by an occasional splash of water, something that is unavoidable when changing the water. Tiles are best in any case. Laminate flooring is not really suitable with an aquarium because unsightly bulges can develop along the joints if you do not wipe up every drop of water right away.

➤ Naturally, the aquarium should not be exposed to excessive tobacco smoke since this could cause the water quality in the tank to deteriorate quickly.

21. **Location:** **Which room in our apartment is best for our new aquarium?**

In principle, you can set up an aquarium in any room of your apartment. Most aquarium owners place their aquarium in the living room, where a large, beautifully planted tank makes an attractive focal point. A comfortable sofa or a cozy seating arrangement invites you to relax in front of the aquarium and watch the fish. A workroom or office is also a suitable spot since watching the fish lets you take frequent, short breaks from your work. An aquarium can also be placed in the bedroom, provided the humming of the filter and the splashing of the water do not disturb your sleep. You can also put an aquarium in a child's room, although your children should be at least ten years old if you set one up there. By that age, most children are sensible enough not to pester the fish or put things into the aquarium that do not belong there. Theoretically, you can even set up an

EXTRA TIP

Breeding setups

If you would like to set up several aquariums or even a small fish room for breeding your fish, I recommend the basement as a suitable location. The room should be tiled if possible and equipped with a water faucet and a drain; then you can change the water easily and quickly.

aquarium in the bathroom. Water changes could certainly be carried out easily there. However, the bathroom in many apartments is small, and space is at a premium there anyway. Besides, the bathroom is seldom a place where you will spend a lot of time watching your fish. Hallways and vestibules are usually busy places and therefore unsuitable locations for an aquarium. The through traffic would be too stressful for the fish.

22. **Moving: I just bought a used aquarium together with all the accessories, equipment, and fish. What is the best way to move it into my apartment?**

➤ First, you should catch all the fish with a fish net and put them in bags for the move. If there are fish in the aquarium that like to hide, like catfish or coolie loaches, proceed as follows. First turn off all the electrical equipment, then carefully remove all the decorations, and finally catch and remove the fish.

➤ Fill as many containers as you can with aquarium water so that the fish will feel at home as quickly as possible after the move.

EXTRA TIP

Transferring aquarium water
Take a hose, fill it with water at the faucet, and close the ends with your thumbs, making sure there is no air in the hose. Now hold one end of the hose in the aquarium water and the other in a container, making sure the container is below the level of the tank. First remove your thumb from the end in the aquarium and then from the end in the container. The water will begin to flow. To stop the flow of water, simply cover the end of the hose in the container.

➤ You can either transport the plants in buckets with enough water to cover them or package them in plastic bags with some water as you did the fish.

➤ Now remove the last of the water from the aquarium, and transfer the substrate to a bucket or sturdy bag.

➤ Remove the electrical equipment next. Be very careful when moving the tank so that it does not crack or break and then spring a leak. The best method is to place the tank in a box lined with pieces of Styrofoam. This way, it is protected from bumps on all sides.

➤ When you arrive home, start by setting the tank on its stand. Then clean it thoroughly, but do not use any chemical cleaners.

➤ Wash the substrate with lukewarm water, and add it to the tank.

Danios and White Cloud
Mountain Minnows
dart about in a
community tank.

➤ Arrange the decorations in the tank, and pour in some of the water you brought along.

➤ Next, put in the plants, add the remaining water from the containers, fill to the desired depth with tap water at the correct temperature, and then switch on the filter and the other electrical equipment.

➤ Finally, float the fish in their bags on the surface of the water for 30–60 minutes so that the temperature in the bags can equalize with that of the aquarium water. Then open the bags, and add some aquarium water to each one. Close them up again. Repeat this every 10 minutes for about one to two hours. At last, you can release the fish into their tank. The move is complete!

23. **Price: I notice that there are large differences in price among ornamental fish. What can I expect to pay for fish?**

Prices for ornamental fish certainly do vary. This depends on the species as well as the appearance of the individual animal. Some of the most expensive fish of all are Koi that have a color pattern that con-

INFO

Captive bred or wild caught?
Some species, although they are bred in captivity in fairly large numbers, are still imported as wild-caught fish; these include discus, many species of catfish, and freshwater rays. Fish that have only scientific names or a C-number or L-number are usually wildcaught. The majority of marine fish are also wild caught. Captive bred fish are better suited for aquarium life than wild caught ones because they are accustomed to aquarium conditions and are more robust.

forms as closely as possible to a particular standard. Champion fish can easily cost hundreds of thousands of dollars. While young Koi can be purchased inexpensively, they are not as perfectly patterned or colored as show-quality fish. Koi can only be kept in an aquarium when young, though; later on they need a garden pond to be really happy.

How much money you'll need to spend for your fish stock naturally depends on the number and kinds of fish you buy. I can only give you a general idea of price for a few popular aquarium fish. You can expect to pay a lot for Discus (*Symphysodon aequifasciatus*) as well as many wild-caught catfish and rays. Depending on the color strain, a beautiful young Discus can cost up to $40; especially unusual colors can cost considerably more.

You can get Cardinal Tetras (*Paracheirodon axelrodii*), Guppies (*Poecilia reticulata*), Swordtails (*Xiphophorus hellerii*), Mollies (*Poecilia sphenops*), Harlequin Rasboras (*Trigonostigma heteromorpha*), or Tiger Barbs (*Puntius tetrazona*) for less than $5.

Somewhat more expensive are Angelfish, which can cost up to $13 depending on the color variety, and Cockatoo Dwarf Cichlids (*Apistogramma cacatuoides*) or Dwarf Gouramis (*Colisa lalia*) for which you can pay up to $10. You can often get a Zebra Danio (*Danio rerio*) for $1. Finally, the price of a fish also depends on where you buy it—whether at a pet store, directly from the breeder, or perhaps at a fish exchange. Aquarists with fish to give away sometimes place small advertisements in the local paper.

If you are new to fish keeping, it is probably best to begin with less expensive species. Cheaper species often require less demanding care, and they are easier to replace should disease or some other serious problem cause trouble in your aquarium.

24. Quarantine: Why must I keep my new fish in quarantine initially?

It is not uncommon for a disease to be introduced into a tank along with apparently healthy new fish. To prevent this, you should keep your new arrivals in a separate quarantine tank for the first two to four weeks. Typically, disease symptoms will appear two to fourteen days after you have purchased the fish. Even if the new arrivals look healthy, they can carry parasites, bacteria, or viruses that may infect the other fish. All of your original fish could get sick or even die if they cannot cope with the pathogens brought in by the new fish. Of course, a quarantine tank does not give you a 100 percent guarantee against the introduction of diseases, but it does reduce the risk considerably.

25. Quarantine: How do I set up a quarantine tank?

A quarantine tank is usually a small tank that is rather sparsely decorated, which means no substrate or plants. To provide hiding places in a quarantine tank, use only decorations that you can disinfect or boil, such as a piece of driftwood or a clay pot. A small filter and a heater complete the setup. Place your new fish into this tank for two to four weeks. Observe the animals and their behavior carefully during this period. When in doubt, have the fish examined by an expert before you add them to your regular aquarium.

If the fish actually do have a disease, they will have to stay in the quarantine tank while they are being treated. They must remain there until you can no longer see any signs of illness. Then you must clean and disinfect the quarantine tank thoroughly, including decorations and equipment, after you move the fish.

26. Renter's Rights: I rent an apartment. Can the landlord prohibit me from setting up an aquarium?

In contrast to the situation with larger pets like dogs and cats, your landlord cannot prohibit you from setting up an aquarium, provided it does not damage the apartment. Fish are considered to be small pets, and keeping them is regarded as conventional use of a rental property. Damage to the apartment is possible if a large, heavy tank exceeds the load-bearing capacity of the floor. Therefore, you should find out how much weight your floor can take before you set up the aquarium.

If you want to have a complete breeding setup with several tanks in your apartment, that might not be viewed as conventional use. In order to avoid problems, you should talk with your landlord before you install breeding facilities like this. The legal situation here is uncertain.

27. Saltwater Aquarium: What is the difference between saltwater and freshwater aquariums, and which is more suitable for me as a beginner?

In a freshwater aquarium, you can generally use tap water, although it often has to be properly conditioned beforehand. A saltwater or marine tank, on the other hand, contains salt water that you have to prepare from completely demineralized water and the appropriate salt mixtures. Although you need a filter and heater for a freshwater aquarium, you must also install a protein skimmer for a saltwater aquarium. If you want to keep other animals like corals along with the saltwater fish, then you need special lighting, as well. Furthermore, many marine fish are more expensive to feed than the standard freshwater fish.

On the whole, considerably more money and effort are needed to buy and maintain a saltwater aquarium than a freshwater aquarium. If you have no experience as an aquarist, you would be better off choosing a freshwater setup. It is true that a saltwater tank with its corals and brilliantly colored fish is very attractive, but you need considerable experience if you want to maintain it successfully for any length of time.

28. Selectively Bred Deformities: I have read that aquarists should not buy fish that have been selectively bred with deformities. What does this mean exactly?

In order to satisfy consumer demand for especially beautiful and unusual fish, breeders are constantly trying to develop new varieties. In some cases, though, selective breeding of certain deformities interferes with the fish's natural behavior.

Goldfish, in particular, come in many different varieties. The variety known as the Lionhead has growths on its head. In extreme cases, these can be so massive that they obscure the eyes and the fish can no longer see. Another variety, called the Bubble-eye, has enormous bubblelike sacks under the eyes that prevent the fish from behaving naturally and digging in the substrate for food. Furthermore, Bubble-eyes must be kept under very special conditions; otherwise their large, extremely delicate eye sacks will be damaged.

Some varieties of Swordtails and Guppies have greatly enlarged fins. In extreme cases, the male's gonopodium (the anal fin that has been transformed into a copulatory organ) no longer functions normally, and these males can no longer reproduce.

Another example of a selectively bred deformity is the so-called Parrotfish, or Blood Parrot Cichlid, which has a highly deformed mouth and a shortened spine. From the viewpoint of animal welfare, you should not buy animals that have been selectively bred with deformities. In many cases, these "designer fish" are very sensitive and susceptible to disease, which is yet another reason to stay away from such animals.

29. Species Names: Why are scientific names used so often when the fish have common names in English?

The scientific name is internationally valid. This means that you can identify any species unambiguously anywhere in the world using the scientific name. That is not the case for the English name. Sometimes the same fish even has different English names. That is why it is standard practice to use the scientific name in species descriptions. You will frequently see the scientific name used in pet stores as well.

30. Species Names: What do the individual parts of the scientific name mean?

The first part of the scientific name is the genus, and the second part is the species. The species name can be derived from the name of the scientific discoverer. For example, *Corydoras rabauti* is named for its discoverer, Rabaut. It can instead reflect characteristics of the fish as in the Tailspot Corydoras, *Corydoras caudimaculatus* (Latin *cauda* = tail, *maculatus* = spotted). Often the original author and the year of the first description are cited as well, for example *Corydoras caudimaculatus*, Rössel 1961. A third component of the name appears if representatives of a species exhibit enough differences to be classified as a subspecies but the differences are not great enough to warrant the creation of a separate species.

31. Transporting Fish: I would like to buy some fish at the pet store. What is the best way to take them home?

When you buy your fish at the pet store, the dealer will properly package them in a plastic bag with rounded corners where the fish cannot get stuck. You should wrap the bag in some newspaper. This keeps the temperature from dropping too much during transport, and it also prevents the fish from being upset by their surroundings. If the trip home will take more than an hour, you should put the plastic bag into an insulated container like a Styrofoam box. This prevents the temperature from rising or falling too much. For shorter trips, a bucket with a tightly fitting lid is also suitable. Make sure that the plastic bag is filled no more than halfway with water; the other half holds air. If there is too much water in the bag, it will not be oxygenated sufficiently during transport.

If you want to transport fish with spines or thorny processes—like those found on many catfish—you should put the first plastic bag inside a second one to be on the safe side. This way, you can prevent all the water from leaking out if a fish punctures the bag.

Once you take possession of your fish, you should get them back to your aquarium as quickly as you can. Do not travel around with them in improvised "aquariums" any longer than is absolutely necessary, as it is not good for their health.

32. **Veterinarian:** **Where can I find the address of a veterinarian who knows a lot about fish?**

Any local veterinary medical society can give you some addresses. There are also lists of addresses on the Internet. Perhaps the veterinarian who treats your other pets can help you or give you the name of a colleague who has experience with fish. You can also ask if anyone at your aquarium club can recommend a fish veterinarian. In the United States, veterinarians are allowed to advertise their services, so you could check magazines and journals for advertisements by veterinarians specializing in fish.

Equipment and Accessories

Your choice of tank, equipment, and plants lays the foundation for good environmental conditions in the aquarium. In the following chapters, you will find answers to questions about equipment, aquascaping, and plant selection.

33. Accessories: Which accessories should I get for my aquarium?

In addition to the essential equipment for the aquarium, I recommend that you get the following items.

➤ Fish net: You can use this to remove fish and plant fragments from the aquarium.

➤ Thermometer: Even though most aquarium water heaters are controlled automatically nowadays, you should still check the water temperature regularly. Thermometers are available in a variety of styles. Whether you choose a liquid thermometer or a digital thermometer depends primarily on how much you want to pay. Whether you use a thermometer that is attached to the inside or outside of the glass or one that floats in the water also makes little difference. All models will give accurate readings. Thermometers that attach to the outside of the aquarium glass use a type of heat-sensitive film and indicate the temperature by different-colored numbers. Thermometers used inside the aquarium are hung from the rim or attached to the inside of the glass with suction cups.

➤ Algae magnet: This makes it easy to clean the aquarium glass. Be careful not to trap little bits of rock or similar materials between the magnet and the glass, though, or you will scratch the glass.

➤ Algae scraper with razor blade: You can remove stubborn algal growth or mineral buildup effortlessly with this tool.

➤ Hose and bucket for changing water changes: The hose should have a siphon starter so that you do not have to use your mouth to start the suction.

➤ Aquarium gravel vacuum: Sinking particles of debris or leftover bits of food are constantly accumulating on the bottom of the aquarium, forming a layer of detritus known as mulm. This can become a breeding ground for bacteria. You can use a gravel vacuum to remove this layer easily without having to drain off the water.

➤ Water tests: You can easily and accurately determine water parameters like pH, hardness, nitrate, nitrite, and ammonia using reagents available at the pet store.

➤ Hose clamps: Having a few hose clamps on hand is useful in case a hose carrying water to or from the tank develops a hole or the external filter starts to leak.

 You can quickly check the water temperature in the tank with the help of a simple thermometer.

34. Aquarium Hood: **What is the purpose of the aquarium hood, and is it absolutely necessary?** **?**

While having a hood on your aquarium is not essential, it does have some advantages. For one thing, a hood prevents the fish from jumping out of the tank. Many species, such as the Splash Tetra (*Copella arnoldi*) and the Marbled Hatchetfish (*Carnegiella strigata*), are excellent jumpers or are easily frightened and try to escape by leaping out of the tank. That often results in the death of the fish, because they asphyxiate on the floor of the room. Apart from this protective function, a hood is also useful because the lighting can be integrated into it. Besides, the water does not evaporate as easily if you cover your aquarium. It also prevents the humidity in your room from being increased unnecessarily. This is especially important if your rooms are rather cool and damp anyway. If the humidity is too high, mold can develop, which is unhealthy.

35. Backgrounds: What options are available for decorating the rear wall of the aquarium?

The pet store offers a large selection of aquarium backgrounds in different styles. Basically, these are either attached to the back of the tank or installed inside the aquarium.

➤ The simplest method of decorating is to tape a plastic sheet printed with a photographic motif—for instance, aquatic plants—to the back of the aquarium. Of course, whether you like standardized scenes like this is a question of individual taste. Make sure, though, that the design fits in with the plants and other decorations in your aquarium; otherwise it will look out of place.

➤ An alternative to the photographic background is a piece of black cardboard or a sheet of cork. Either can be attached to the back of the aquarium. A black background makes the colors of the fish and the green of the plants stand out especially. A sheet of cork, in contrast, gives your aquarium a certain natural look.

This realistic reproduction of a rocky wall is made of synthetic material and is available at the pet store.

The decorative root used here as an aquarium backdrop is not real, either, but rather a plastic reproduction.

➤ Even more realistic are three-dimensional tank inserts that you can fasten to the rear wall of the aquarium. Simple, low-relief models are especially suitable for narrow tanks because they take away very little space from the front.

➤ Artistically crafted backgrounds made of synthetic materials are very attractive and provide detailed reproductions of natural objects, for instance a root or a rock face. These elements jut out into the aquarium, creating a feeling of depth. Keep in mind, though, that backgrounds like this displace a greater volume of water than flat ones, reducing the total water volume in your tank. Backgrounds that are installed inside the aquarium must, of course, be attached securely with aquarium silicone sealant.

➤ Some aquarists design their own backdrops using rigid foam sheets. If you intend to do this, make sure not to contaminate the water with substances that could poison the fish.

36. Backgrounds: Is having a background for my aquarium absolutely necessary, or can I do without it?

Theoretically, you can omit the background. This is even recommended if you are setting up your aquarium as a room divider and would like to view it from all sides.

However, most aquarium owners install a background for tanks that are set up in front of a wall. This makes sense for aesthetic reasons. If you look at an aquarium and the first thing you see is the flowered wallpaper behind it, then even the most attractively designed underwater landscape will not look its best. Besides, a more realistic background will give your fish a greater sense of feeling at home in their environment. And more content fish are healthier fish.

37. **Basic Equipment: I would like to get my first aquarium. What equipment is absolutely necessary for the fish and plants to thrive?**

A heater, lights, and a filter are essential for an aquarium to function properly. A heater is necessary because normal room temperature is too low for most tropical freshwater fish. An aquarium filter keeps the water free of coarse particulates and breaks down organic wastes. Without sufficient light, your aquarium plants will not grow.

Apart from this basic equipment, there are some other accessories you could use, depending on your type of aquarium. These include an automatic feeder, an airstone, and a UV sterilizer.

In any case, I suggest you have a diaphragm air pump on hand. There are always situations in which a pump like this is helpful, for instance if the filter breaks down or you need to provide additional oxygen. You will need an air pump in the quarantine tank, anyway, for supplemental aeration when you are treating the fish with medications. Depending on the model, you may also need the pump for your gravel vacuum.

38. **Buying a Used Tank: Is buying a used tank a good idea?**

The advantage of buying a used aquarium from a private individual is that it is usually much less expensive than a new one. However, you have no guarantee that the tank is free from defects and will not start to leak before long. If, on the other hand, you get a new aquarium at the pet store, the dealer will guarantee it against leaks. Besides, with a used tank, you never know what went on in it beforehand. Were the previous occupants healthy? A used tank can harbor disease-causing organisms if it was not disinfected properly. That is why you should always disinfect a used aquarium before you start to set it up.

If you are new to the fish-keeping hobby, it is a good idea to go with a new aquarium. Buying a used aquarium is best left to more experienced aquarists who can spot and take care of potential problems more quickly and easily. You do not want your first experience with an aquarium to be a bad one.

39. Cycling the Filter: What does it mean to cycle the filter?

A new filter normally takes several weeks to be colonized sufficiently by the bacteria that break down harmful wastes. Only after this maturation period, a process commonly referred to as conditioning or cycling, does filter performance reach its peak.

During this time, levels of certain toxic substances like nitrite or ammonia can rise rapidly, possibly harming or even killing the fish. The filter bacteria, however, need these nitrogenous compounds in the water as a food source.

This is why you should not put any fish into the aquarium at the beginning of the cycling process. Instead, add a few snails, and feed them small amounts of dry food.

After about two or three weeks, you can put in a few fish, which you should likewise feed rather sparingly. Once there is a sufficiently large population of bacteria (usually after three to four weeks), the filter is able to process the accumulating organic wastes. Then you can add more fish.

During the entire cycling period, you should test the water parameters every two to three days, especially the pH, nitrite, nitrate, and ammonia levels. This way you can act quickly if the levels rise high enough to present a threat to the fish. Remember, the health of your fish depends on your willingness to monitor aquarium conditions.

BASIC EQUIPMENT

Having the proper basic equipment is essential for successful fish keeping. You will find a wide assortment to choose from at the pet store: filters, heaters, lighting units, aeration

INTERNAL FILTER

This is placed into the tank and, depending on the type, can be operated by a diaphragm air pump or a motor-driven pump. Internal filters are especially good for small tanks with only a few fish.

EXTERNAL FILTER

Because of its high-capacity filter canister, this type is ideal for large aquariums. Some external filters, called thermofilters, have an integrated heater that warms the water as it flows through the filter.

AUTOMATIC AQUARIUM WATER HEATER

Modern aquarium heaters are thermostatically controlled and can be adjusted over a range of temperatures. The heater should shut off automatically if it is not fully submersed or if it is defective.

devices, and automatic feeders. Learn as much as you can, and then decide what will be useful for your aquarium.

LIGHTING
It simulates a natural day-night rhythm for fish and plants. Proper lighting creates a pleasant environment for your aquarium community and accentuates the effect of a beautifully aquascaped tank.

AUTOMATIC FEEDER
An automatic feeder is especially useful for feeding the fish while you are on vacation. It dispenses food into the aquarium at regular intervals over an extended period of time so the fish do not have to go hungry.

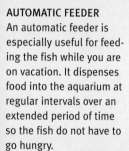

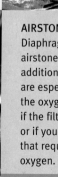

AIRSTONE
Diaphragm pumps and airstones provide additional oxygen. They are especially useful when the oxygen level is low, if the filter malfunctions, or if you are keeping fish that require a lot of oxygen.

40. **Cycling the Filter: Are there any ways to reduce the amount of time needed to cycle a new filter?**

One way you can speed up the cycling process is with bacterial cultures available from the pet store. Another method that works quite well is to inoculate the new filter with media from a mature filter. Obviously, this material must come from a well-maintained tank in which there are no pathogens. Otherwise, you run the risk of introducing disease into your tank.

41. **Decorations: Why are decorations necessary in an aquarium?**

The right decorations can give the aquarium a natural appearance. However, decorations are not just important for aesthetic reasons; they are also necessary for the well-being of the fish. For example, halved coconut shells and drift-

The filter breaks down toxic wastes.

wood, in addition to being attractive, provide good
spawning sites for cave brooders. Decorative wood is
essential in a tank with catfish because many species,
such as bristlenose catfish, need cellulose and get it by
rasping away at the wood.

**42. Decorations: Which objects and materials can
be used in the aquarium?**

You can use the following materials as decorations
in your aquarium: wood, halved coconut shells from
which you have removed the flesh, bamboo, and
rocks. The rocks, of course, cannot be calcareous. Use
aquarium silicone sealant to glue together rock structures so that they do not come tumbling down and
possibly injure the fish. Because of the risk of injury,
you should avoid holey rock with very sharp edges.

INFO

Aquarium silicone sealant

Whenever you need silicone sealant for working in your aquarium, be sure to use the special aquarium-grade sealant that
you can get at the pet store. Never use the silicone sealant
sold in home improvement centers; this type contains antifungal and antibacterial additives that could be toxic to your
aquarium fish. Clay flowerpots also make interesting decorations for your aquarium. Whether to use plastic decorations is
a question of personal taste. In my opinion, plastic skulls or
pirates are kitsch and do not belong in an aquarium that is,
after all, supposed to reproduce a natural scene. On the other
hand, you can design lovely underwater landscapes using artificial driftwood. A word of caution—some plastic decorations
contain high levels of plasticizers, which can harm the fish.
You also have to be careful with colored sand and colored
rocks. They can release substances that will quickly and dra-
matically alter some water parameters.

43. Decorations: Are bamboo canes safe to use as decorations in the aquarium?

In principle, you can decorate your aquarium with bamboo canes. Keep in mind, though, that they are most effective when arranged in groups with the individual canes placed vertically and parallel to each other. Because they are very light, bamboo canes float very easily. If you just stick them into the substrate, they will soon be scattered all over the aquarium. Therefore, you have to weigh down the canes and anchor them to the bottom. In addition, you should seal the open ends with aquarium silicone sealant so that they do not start to decay and foul the water in your tank. Incidentally, when properly anchored and laid horizontally on the substrate, bamboo canes are readily used as hiding places and spawning caves by aquarium fish like Peacock Gobies (*Tateurndina ocellicauda*) and some suckermouth armored catfish.

44. Duration of Lighting: How many hours per day should an aquarium be illuminated?

Most ornamental fish and aquatic plants are native to tropical waters. Because the tropics are close to the equator, the sun shines there between 12 and 14 hours a day. For this reason, I recommend that you leave your aquarium lights on for this length of time, too.

45. Fertilizing Plants: My aquarium plants are not growing well. Should I give them aquarium plant fertilizer regularly?

Normally, aquatic plants will grow in an aquarium stocked with fish even without regular fertilization.

The fish produce enough organic matter to nourish the plants. Sometimes an iron deficiency develops, but it is easily treated with the proper iron supplement. Fertilization with carbon dioxide promotes plant growth in general. For aquariums with plants but no fish (known as Dutch aquariums) and very densely planted aquariums, fertilize regularly with special aquarium plant supplements. Otherwise, a nutrient deficiency can easily develop. In general, adding fertilizer once every four weeks is sufficient. Check the manufacturer's instructions on the fertilizer package for information on dosage and frequency of fertilization.

Be careful not to overfertilize your aquarium. If you provide too much of a good thing, excessive growth of unwanted algae can result. Algae, after all, need the same nutrients as the other plants; however, they reproduce much faster.

46. Fertilizing Plants: I would like to add carbon dioxide to my aquarium to fertilize the plants. How do I do this?

There are various methods for supplying an aquarium with CO_2.

One new device is the Carbonator, a small container that is placed directly into the aquarium. Inside the container is a cartridge containing harmless chemical substances that react with each other to produce CO_2.

Carbonators do not need electricity or pressurized gas bottles. However, they have one major disadvantage: You cannot regulate the amount of CO_2 released into the aquarium. You also have to change the cartridge every four to eight weeks.

For this reason, most aquarists prefer CO_2 fertilization systems in which the CO_2 is introduced into the aquarium through a tube from a pressurized gas bottle. A pressure regulator on the CO_2 bottle allows you to control the dosage of carbon dioxide.

AQUASCAPING MATERIALS

Attractive aquascaping is not just aesthetically appealing. It also gives structure to the aquarium space, provides the fish with hiding places, and acts as a substrate for

BAMBOO CANES
Bamboo can be used unvarnished. However, bamboo is very buoyant, even if it has been soaked for a long time. For this reason, anchor sections of bamboo with a rock so that they stay on the bottom.

WOOD
A wide variety of decorative wood is available at the pet store. Wood collected from bogs, like bogwood roots or Scottish bog oak, is especially good. It will not decompose and is heavier than water.

LEAF LITTER
A thick layer of dead leaves (for example, beech or oak) will simulate the natural habitat of fish, especially in biotope aquariums like this blackwater tank.

epiphytic plants. Pet stores carry some excellent materials for aquascaping. Here is a small sample.

ROCKS
These should generally be lime free and smooth edged. Pieces of slate and sandstone are especially good. When decorating with rocks, make sure to leave enough room for the fish to swim.

HOLEY ROCK

This calcareous rock, also called honeycomb limestone, is ideal for aquariums with hardwater fish from Central America and East Africa. Be careful not to concentrate too much weight at just a few points on the glass bottom of the aquarium.

COCONUT SHELLS
Fish will happily take up residence in halved coconut shells or an entire shell with a large hole bored in it. Boil the shells first so they are completely waterlogged and do not float.

47. Filter: What is the function of filtration, and what types of filters are available?

Operating an aquarium without good filtration is impossible. The function of filtration is to rid the water of visible as well as invisible impurities.

There are three different types of filtration: mechanical, biological, and chemical. Different filter media are used for each of these processes.

You have a choice of two filter types. External filters are located outside the aquarium and are connected to the tank with hoses. Internal filters, on the other hand, are placed directly into the tank.

48. Filter Malfunction: What should I do if my filter breaks down over the weekend?

For an emergency like this, you should have a diaphragm air pump that you can hook up to a small, inexpensive plastic box filter or an airstone. This way you can at least keep the water moving and ensure that the tank is supplied with oxygen. It is even better if you get a small internal filter as a backup. If necessary, you can then use this for a rearing tank or even for the quarantine tank. Just remember, though, that the quarantine tank and its accessories must always be cleaned and disinfected if sick fish are treated in it. You should never remove anything from a quarantine tank and use it in another tank without first taking these precautions.

So that you can act quickly when faced with filter problems, I suggest you ask the pet store dealer which parts of your filter are most likely to wear out. The answer varies depending on the make and model. Always keep replacements for these parts on hand, because once you spot a problem with the filter, you must take action to solve it quickly. Otherwise, the water in your aquarium will rapidly become toxic to your fish.

49. Filter Media: Which filter media are available, and what effect do they have?

A filter removes particles of debris from the water and breaks down harmful substances by means of mechanical, biological, and chemical filtration processes. A variety of media are used in these processes. You can get all these filter media at the pet store.

➤ Biological filtration relies on bacteria that colonize the filter media and convert harmful waste products into less-harmful substances. The greater the surface area of a filter medium, the more beneficial bacteria can colonize it and the more it cleans the water by

HOW FILTER MEDIA WORK

Material	Filter Medium Mechanical Filtration	Biological Filtration	Comments
Sand and gravel	+++	+	Material should be calcium free
Foam	+++	++	Use only special filter foam from the pet store
Bio-balls	+	+++	Especially for filters with a large filter chamber
Sintered media	+	+++	Extremely large surface area for colonization by filter bacteria
Filter floss	+++	++	Comes in a variety of textures (coarse to fine)
Activated carbon	+	++	Removes chemical substances from the water

Effectiveness: + low, ++ good, +++ high

biological filtration. Biological and mechanical filtration are coupled to a greater or lesser degree since bacteria can colonize the surface of any filter medium.

➤ In mechanical filtration, coarse particles of debris are removed from the water and retained in the filter. These particles are washed away during regular cleaning of the filter media. Sand and gravel are two media that can be used for coarse mechanical filtration. Filter floss is one of the classic mechanical filter media and is made of either fine or coarse fibers. Other filter media used for mechanical filtration are perforated plastic filter media balls (called bio-balls), granular materials, and foam. These all have a large surface area, which makes them important in biological filtration processes, as well.

➤ Filter media used for chemical filtration include peat and activated carbon. Peat is suitable for softening the water, lowering the pH, and adding humic acid to the water. Peat is used in the aquarium by adding it to a separate filter chamber in the existing filter system or by putting it into a separate filter. Use only special peat intended for the aquarium. Do not use garden peat, because it contains fertilizers. Add peat to only moderately hard or hard water and leave it in the filter for no longer that one to two weeks. Otherwise, it will decay and foul the water. Activated carbon is suitable for filtering out many chemical substances. You can use activated carbon to remove a yellowish tinge from the water or to eliminate drug residues after medicating the tank.

Never use activated carbon while you are using medications, though, because it will filter out the medications and render the treatment ineffective. The adsorption capacity of activated carbon is limited. It should therefore be used for only a few days at a time and then removed; otherwise the substances that it filtered out will be released back into the water again.

50. Filter Noise: My aquarium is in my bedroom. The noise of the filter disturbs me when I'm trying to get to sleep. Can I switch off the filter at night?

Never switch off the filter at night. This could lead to oxygen deficiency in the filter, and the bacteria that break down toxic wastes could die as a result. Stopping the filter for even an hour harms the bacteria and impairs filter performance. After an interruption of just a few hours, a smelly brew develops in the filter. If the filter is then switched back on, the toxins that have built up in the filter pose a real danger to the fish. If your filter happens to fail, you must rinse the filter contents thoroughly with lukewarm water before you start it up again.

If the noise disturbs you, then you should buy a filter that runs quietly. With some external filters, you can even put a pad under the filter canister to dampen the sound. If you also make sure the filter outlet is at or below the water surface, this will prevent the water from splashing as it returns to the tank. If none of this helps, you will just have to put the aquarium into another room.

51. Filter Performance: I want to buy a new filter for my aquarium. What sort of output should a filter have?

Which filter is right for you depends on a variety of factors. How large is your tank? How frequent and how large are your water changes? How many fish are in you tank? Do you want an external or an internal filter?

If you have a 25-gallon (100 L) tank with few fish and plenty of plants, feed the fish sparingly, and carry out regular water changes, you can get by with a less-powerful filter than if you have a 15-gallon (60 L) tank with lots of fish, very few plants, heavy feeding, and irregular partial water changes.

As a general rule, the greater the filter output, the better. Aquariums containing plants only (Dutch aquariums) are an exception, and they should be filtered rather gently. For a sparsely to normally stocked aquarium, half of the water volume should be filtered per hour. In addition, the filter canister should be able to hold at least 1 quart (1 L) of filter medium per 25 gallons (100 L) of tank water. The larger the filter canister is in relation to the water volume, the more effective the filtration.

52. **Filter Performance: How can I determine the actual output of an aquarium filter?**

You can determine the output of your filter quite simply, although it is usually given on the filter or in the instruction manual. Of course, peak performance is achieved only if the filter media are loosely packed and clean. For this reason, I suggest that you actually measure the flow rate of your filter. To do this, you need a bucket, a measuring cup, and a stopwatch. Hold the bucket under the filter outlet for exactly 60 seconds. Use the measuring cup to determine the volume of water you collected. Multiply this volume in gallons (liters) by 60, and you will know how many gallons (liters) of water are filtered per hour.

Because filter performance declines sharply as debris accumulates, you have to clean the filter regularly. Failure to do so can cause serious problems in water quality, which, in turn, can cause serious health problems among your fish. Be sure to develop a routine filter-maintenance schedule.

53. Filter Types: The pet store carries internal and external filters. What are the advantages and disadvantages of an external filter?

External filters come in different sizes. They are suitable for small tanks as well as for larger ones and are set up outside the aquarium. Your aquarium dealer should be able to give you useful suggestions about which particular external filter is most suitable for your aquarium. The most elegant solution is to house the filter in the aquarium cabinet.

➤ **Advantages:** External filters usually have a relatively large filter canister and, consequently, a longer service life than internal filters. Service life is defined as the length of time a filter can function until the next maintenance or cleaning.

As a result, a proper-sized external filter will need to be cleaned less often than an internal filter in the same tank. Its performance is usually much better, too, since it will hold large amounts of different types of filter media. Because of this, extensive biological filtration of the water occurs in an external filter once it has finished cycling.

➤ **Disadvantages:** The major disadvantage is that they take more effort to clean than internal filters. The filter hoses must be emptied and clamped. In addition, the filter media take longer to clean because an external filter holds more than an internal filter.

You can make your task easier if you equip the hoses with double disconnect valves. When you have finished cleaning, make sure that no air bubbles remain in the filter canister after the water is drawn in. Otherwise, filter performance will be impaired. Ask your pet store dealer for a filter equipped with a bleeder valve that prevents this sort of problem.

Filter performance is crucial to the health of your fish, so make sure that you have the most efficient equipment for your aquarium.

54. Filter Types: When is an internal filter useful?

If your aquarium is located on a shelf or a table, an internal filter is certainly better than an external filter for aesthetic reasons. An internal filter is not suitable for large tanks because it has less filter capacity. However, an internal filter takes up a lot of space, especially in a small tank, and it has to be cleaned frequently because of its small filter volume.

55. Floating Plants: Is using floating plants in the aquarium a good idea, or do they disturb the fish?

Far from disturbing the fish, floating plants offer them several advantages. The plants provide welcome places to lay eggs and good hiding places for baby fish. In addition, they compete with troublesome algae. Floating plants also subdue very bright

Water Lettuce is one of the most popular floating plants.

aquarium lighting, which suits fish like bristlenose catfish that prefer rather low light.

Suitable floating plants include Salvinia (*Salvinia natans*), Crystalwort (*Riccia fluitans*), and Water Lettuce (*Pistia stratiotes*). Although fish have no problems with floating plants, other aquarium plants can suffer because of them. Make sure that the floating plants never cover more than a third of the water surface. Otherwise, plants deeper in the tank will not receive enough light and may become stunted.

If duckweed gets into the aquarium, it can grow rampantly and become a nuisance.

56. Heating: What options are available for heating an aquarium?

Automatic aquarium water heaters that are installed in the aquarium are the most common and, based on the ratio of price to performance, the best. They are regulated by a thermostat and maintain a constant temperature in the aquarium. Automatic aquarium heaters are available at the pet store in a variety of wattages for practically any size aquarium.

External filters with integrated heaters (thermo-filters) are also available. They supply the tank with evenly warmed water so no additional heat source needs to be installed in the aquarium. The disadvantage of such two-in-one devices, though, is that you always have to replace both components—the filter and the heater—even if only one is defective. Systems like this are also more likely to malfunction.

You can also maintain the aquarium water at a constant temperature using substrate heating. For this purpose, you can either place an undertank heating pad beneath the aquarium or bury a heating cable in the substrate. Plants respond especially well to this sort of substrate heating. However, replacing these heat sources is difficult and very expensive if they ever develop problems.

57. **Heating: What wattage should an aquarium heater have?**

The required wattage can be estimated as follows. If the aquarium is located in an unheated room, then figure on approximately 4 watts per gallon (1 watt per liter) of water. On the other hand, if it is in a heated room, you can estimate 1–2 watts per gallon (0.3–0.5 watts per liter). Thus for an aquarium with 45 gallons (180 L) of water located in an unheated room, you would need a 180-watt heater. If it is in a heated room, you would need a heater rated at 54–90 watts. For very large tanks measuring 48 inches (120 cm) or more in length, you should install two heaters with half the wattage each. This prevents the devices from wearing out too quickly and reduces the danger of overheating. I suggest you check the temperature daily using a thermometer. This way you will immediately notice if a heater stops working or overheats, and you can then act quickly.

58. **Ion Exchanger: What is an ion exchanger, and when is it necessary?**

An ion exchanger is a device that completely demineralizes the water by using synthetic resins to replace anions (negatively charged ions) and cations (positively charged ions) with OH^- or H^+ ions. In simple terms, you could say that it replaces dissolved salts (which are responsible for water hardness) with pure water. Using an ion exchange unit makes sense if you have very hard tap water but want to keep fish that require soft water, such as Discus.

You also need demineralized water if you have an open tank and want to replace the water lost through evaporation.

59. Leaky Aquarium: What can I do if the aquarium springs a leak over the weekend and the water starts to drain out?

To be prepared for a situation like this, you should always keep a small spare tank on hand where you can transfer the fish in a hurry. In an emergency, even a plastic tub from the home improvement center will work. Fill your temporary tank with as much of the water remaining in the aquarium as possible so that the transition to new water parameters will not be too stressful for your fish. Transfer the filter from the leaky aquarium to the spare tank. Be sure not to switch it off, or the filter bacteria will die and the aquarium will have to go through the whole cycling process again. This way, your filter can continue to work at full efficiency, and you can use it for your repaired tank or a new tank. I suggest you always keep a tube of aquarium silicone sealant on hand so that you can quickly repair small defects in the tank your-self. If the tank is an older one in which the silicone has become brittle, then buy a new tank.

EXTRA TIP

Keep a spare tank handy
I recommend that you always have a spare tank on hand in case your aquarium leaks and you have to transfer your fish to another tank quickly. The best thing for this purpose is a small 15-gallon (60 L) tank. An aquarium like this is also useful as a quarantine tank for new arrivals or sick fish. Do not forget to equip this spare tank with a small filter and a heater, too.

60. Lighting: Why does an aquarium need lights?

For one thing, lighting is essential for aquarium plants to survive and grow. Photosynthesis can occur only if sufficient light is available. In this biochemical process, plant cells produce organic substances and oxygen from carbon dioxide and water in the presence of light. Plants release the oxygen into the water, which is beneficial for the fish. If you leave the lights on for about 12–14 hours per day for your tropical fish and then switch them off at night, you will simulate the natural alternation of day and night. The more closely you reproduce the natural environment of your fish in the aquarium, the happier they will be.

In addition, good lighting brings out the beauty of the fish. If an unlit aquarium is simply placed near a window, the sunlight entering from the side usually makes the fish look pale and transparent. Besides, placing the aquarium near a window like this will result in excessive growth of algae.

61. Measuring Water Parameters: How can I measure the water parameters in my aquarium?

The best way to measure the water parameters is with test strips or liquid test kits available at the pet store.

Test strips are very simple to use. The strip is dipped into the water, and the result can be read after a brief interval. The levels of substances being tested can usually be determined using a color scale.

With liquid test kits, you add a specific number of drops to a small test tube containing aquarium water. Depending on the test, you may have to add a second reagent. When you compare the color of the water with a color scale, you can determine the level of a specific substance in the aquarium water. Of course, measurements made using test strips or liquid test kits are not as precise as laboratory analyses. In most cases, though, they are adequate.

Electronic devices are also available for measuring some water parameters, such as the pH meter used to determine pH. However, this equipment is relatively expensive and has to be calibrated at regular intervals. Devices like this are normally not necessary for the aquarium hobbyist.

Many pet dealers will also analyze your water. If you would like to have a very precise analysis, you can send a water sample to a laboratory. These analyses are very accurate. Because of the labor and the high-tech laboratory equipment involved, they are relatively expensive.

62. **Open Tanks: What are the advantages of an aquarium that is open on top?**

Actually, the only advantage of an open-topped aquarium is aesthetic, because open tanks are usually very decorative. One way to provide lighting for an open aquarium is with a pendant, or hanging, lamp. However, you should use only hanging lamps equipped with a splash guard. The plants in an open aquarium can grow up above the water surface, which looks very attractive. Naturally, an aquarium without

Open-topped aquariums look very attractive. You need a cover, though, if your fish like to jump.

a cover increases the humidity in the room. If it is in a room with very dry air, this can improve the indoor climate. You always have to replace evaporated water with demineralized water. You should not use tap water because this would permanently increase the hardness of the aquarium water. Eventually, the water hardness limit would be exceeded, especially for soft-water fish. Whether you decide on an open-topped or a covered aquarium should depend on your fish. An aquarium cover is a necessity if you have species that like to jump. You also have to consider the climate in you room. Naturally, the decision is also a question of personal taste.

63. Planting: What is the right way to put plants into the substrate?

Plant your aquarium plants as soon as possible after buying them. If you are setting up a new tank, first mix the substrate with the nutrient-rich granular planting medium according to the manufacturer's instructions on the product packaging. Then fill the tank with water to a depth of about 4–8 inches (10–20 cm). Now take the plants out of their bag and remove everything that is not part of the plant.

EXTRA TIP

Snail eggs on aquarium plants
Before you put your new plants into the aquarium, examine them carefully for small, aquatic snails as well as snail eggs. If you discover any of the jellylike eggs, you should first place the plants into a separate container for a few days and add a snail control product (from the pet store) to the water. This will kill both the snails and their eggs so that you do not introduce any unwelcome "guests."

Then trim back the roots to about half their original length using a sharp pair of scissors; this will encourage the growth of new roots. Next, rinse the plants under lukewarm running water to remove any material clinging to them. To set in the plants, poke a hole in the substrate with one finger and place the roots into it. Then spread some substrate over the roots and press it down firmly around the plant. If the water level is still too low, carefully add more to fill the tank.

64. **Plants: I would like my aquarium to be very heavily planted. Is that possible, and what should I keep in mind if I do it?**

You can indeed set up an underwater garden. However, you should put as few fish as possible into a heavily planted aquarium and choose species that will not harm the plants. Naturally, you should not select fish that need a lot of open space to swim. Suitable fish include Redchin Panchax (*Epiplatys dageti*), Siamese Fighting Fish (*Betta splendens*), and Striped Panchax (*Aplocheilus lineatus*). If you also pay attention to the following guidelines, your plants will be sure to thrive.

➤ Filter flow: It should not be too strong because many plants do not like that.

Plants supply the tank with oxygen as well as provide hiding places and spawning sites for the fish.

➤ Lighting: Make sure the light intensity—from 2–4 watts per gallon (0.5–1 watt per liter)—and light spectrum are appropriate for plants. The spectrum should have a high proportion of blue and red light. You can buy fluorescent bulbs especially designed to promote plant growth.

➤ Carbon dioxide fertilization: The introduction of carbon dioxide encourages plant growth.

➤ Plant fertilizers: Add aquarium plant fertilizer regularly in order to provide the plants with the necessary nutrients.

65. Plastic Plants: I would prefer to use plastic plants rather than real ones in my aquarium. Will that work?

Live plants perform important functions that artificial plants cannot. Live plants remove substances from the water that could harm the fish, especially nitrogen compounds and phosphates. In addition, when exposed to light, live plants produce the oxygen that fish need to live. Many fish also like to nibble on aquatic plants, which are a welcome vegetable supplement to their diet. Last but not least, a beautifully planted aquarium is a marvelous sight.

Whether live or plastic, plants offer hiding places for fish, including baby fish. In addition, fish like Angelfish and Rams like to lay their eggs on the leaves. Of course, some fish are very hard on plants, making it difficult to have a planted tank. For example, many larger cichlids pull the plants apart in no time. In this case, you can buy only extremely hardy plants like Dwarf Anubias (*Anubias barteri* var. *nana*) or else just get plastic plants. Make sure, though, that they do not contain any plasticizers, because these can harm the fish.

66. Propagating Plants: Can I propagate aquarium plants myself?

Yes, you can propagate most aquarium plants yourself.

Many plants can be propagated by cutting off runners. Runners are daughter plants that grow on the ends of rootlike shoots. This type of propagation works relatively well for plants like vallisneria (*Vallisneria* spp.). Smaller *Echinodorus* species like the Bolivian Swordplant (*Echinodorus bolivianus*) can also be propagated using runners.

With other species, for example *Elodea*, an independent, fully developed plant can grow from a piece of stem. All you have to do is stick the fragment of stem into the substrate, where it will produce its own roots. This is known as propagation from cuttings.

Another type of propagation uses so-called adventitious plantlets, which are young plants that form directly on the parent plant. Simply separate the babies from the parent and plant them in the substrate. This method is used for Indian Fern (*Ceratopteris thalictroides*) as well as some *Echinodorus* species in which the plantlets develop on inflorescences.

67. Pruning Plants: Is it necessary to prune aquarium plants?

Once a month, you should use a sharp pair of scissors to trim back the stems of aquarium plants that have grown too long; otherwise they will develop bare spots. If there is too little swimming space for the fish or if the stems are growing out of the water so that their upper leaves are being scorched by the lights, you should prune these plants back severely. When you do this, however, always be sure to leave at least two pairs of leaves above the substrate so that the plant can continue to photosynthesize. It looks more natural if you do not trim back a group of plants horizontally to all the same height but instead leave the plants in the center a little taller than those on the edges.

68. Replacing the Lights: When must I replace the bulbs in my aquarium to be sure that all the plants and animals in it are getting enough light?

You should not wait until fluorescent bulbs start to flicker or burn out before replacing them. I recommend that you replace the fluorescent bulbs every six to eight months, or after 12 months at the latest, because then the light output drops off substantially. Do not replace all the bulbs at once, though. Not all plants will tolerate a sudden change like this and may lose their leaves.

Metal halide bulbs (HQI) should be replaced every nine months. For mercury vapor lamps (HQL), it is sufficient to replace the bulbs about every 12 months.

69. Rocks: Is there any problem with using rocks from a lake to decorate my aquarium?

If the rocks are not calcium free, then they can certainly be used for decorating an aquarium. You can easily test a rock to see if it contains calcium. If you put a few drops of 3 percent hydrochloric acid (from the pharmacy) onto a rock or sand, it will begin to foam if it is calcareous.

If you want to use a rock that you have found in a natural body of water, you should not only test it for calcium but you should also boil it before you put it into the aquarium. That prevents fish diseases or unwelcome hitchhikers like freshwater polyps (hydras), flatworms (planarians), nematodes, and leeches from being introduced into the aquarium.

70. Selecting Plants: What should I keep in mind when selecting plants for my aquarium?

Your selection depends upon a variety of factors.

► Tank size: In a small tank, you should generally use plants that stay small. You can put in just one large specimen plant as a special focal point, perhaps a Madagascar Lace Plant (*Aponogeton madagascariensis*).

► Light intensity: Plants have different requirements for light. Some, like swordplants (*Echinodorus* spp.), need high light intensity, while others, like cryptocorynes (*Cryptocoryne* sp.), get by with less light.

► Water quality: Many water plants grow better in soft, slightly acidic water than in hard, alkaline water. Consequently, water parameters will also influence your selection of suitable plants.

► Fish stock: Some fish are plant eaters and nibble on the leaves. In this case, choose vigorous, robust species and avoid fine-leaved plants.

► Foreground and background: There should be plenty of swimming room in the foreground. Here you can use low-growing plants that will form a dense carpet, like Dwarf Sagittaria (*Sagittaria subulata f. pusilla*), Tiny Cryptocoryne (*Cryptocoryne parva*), or Pygmy Chain Swordplant (*Echinodorus tenellus*). Suitable plants for the background, on the other hand, are tall species like Giant Hygrophila (*Hygrophila corymbosa*) or Ruffled Aponogeton (*Aponogeton crispus*).

If you are not sure about the best plants to include in your aquarium, you should consult an expert, like an aquarium store owner. He or she should be able to give you useful advice on how to stock your aquarium with plants.

PLANTS FOR THE AQUARIUM

NAME	TYPE	HEIGHT in inches (cm)	TEMPER-ATURE °F (°C)	PLACEMENT
Amazon Swordplant (*Echinodorus amazonicus*)	Rosette	12–20 (30–50)	72–82 (22–28)	Specimen plant or in small groups, background
Wendt's Cryptocoryne (*Cryptocoryne wendtii*)	Rosette	4–12 (10–30)	72–80 (22–26)	Middle ground
Lake Biwa Vallisneria (*Vallisneria* sp.)	Rosette	up to 16 (40)	72–82 (22–28)	Middle ground and background
Floating Arrowhead (*Sagittaria subulata*)	Rosette	up to 4 (10)	64–82 (18–28)	Foreground and middle ground
Dwarf Hygrophila (*Hygrophila polysperma*)	Stem	up to 20 (50)	68–82 (20–28)	Middle ground and background
Giant Elodea (*Egeria densa*)	Stem	20–32 (50–80)	59–77 (15–25)	As a group in the middle ground or background
Water Wisteria (*Hygrophila difformis*)	Stem	12–28 (30–70)	74–82 (23–28)	Middle ground and background
Java Fern (*Microsorium pteropus*) .	Epiphyte	up to 12 (30)	72–82 (22–28)	Tied to rocks or driftwood
Java Moss (*Vesicularia dubyana*)	Epiphyte	up to 6 (15)	59–86 (15–30)	Tied to rocks or driftwood
Hornwort (*Ceratophyllum demersum*)	Free floating	6–40 (15–100)	68–82 (20–28)	Everywhere
Crystalwort (*Riccia fluitans*)	Floating plant	—	59–86 (15–30)	Water surface
Water Lettuce (*Pistia stratiotes*)	Floating plant	—	72–86 (22–30)	Water surface

71. Selecting Plants: **Which aquarium plants are recommended and easy to care for?**

The following plants are relatively robust and usually available throughout the year from your pet dealer.

➤ Rosette-forming swordplants (*Echinodorus* sp.) are available in a variety of sizes. They are very robust but require plenty of light.

➤ Various species of hygrophila (*Hygrophila* sp.) have a stemlike growth habit and usually grow quickly.

➤ Cryptocorynes (*Cryptocoryne* sp.) can grow under low light but prefer soft water.

➤ Indian Fern (*Ceratopteris thalictroides*) and Java Fern (*Microsorium pteropus*) are very vigorous. You can easily propagate them using the adventitious plantlets on the leaves.

➤ Vallisneria (*Vallisneria* sp.) has straplike leaves and can form attractive groups by means of runners. These plants prefer water that is not too soft.

➤ Fine-leaved hornworts (*Ceratophyllum* sp.) can be anchored in the substrate, but they normally drift freely in the water and can form dense clumps.

If these plants are not suitable for your aquarium for one reason or another, seek out an expert for further suggestions. Also, be sure to avoid plants that are not suitable for your aquarium.

INFO

Unsuitable plants
Some plants are completely unsuitable for use in an aquarium, since they will die very quickly under water. Here are a few examples: *Aglaonema, Caladium,* Spider Plant, *Cordyline, Dieffenbachia, Dracaena, Fittonia,* Polka Dot Plant, *Peliosanthes, Philodendron,* Artillery Plant, Devil's Ivy, Spikemoss.

72. Substrate: What is the function of the substrate in an aquarium?

The substrate performs several functions in an aquarium. It provides a place for the plant roots to take hold and supplies them with the necessary nutrients. In addition, it is colonized by bacteria that break down harmful waste products, which is important for water quality. Bottom-dwelling fish also dig through the substrate looking for food.

73. Substrate: What do I have to take into consideration when selecting the substrate?

➤ The substrate should not contain any sharp-edged pieces that could hurt the fish. Callichthyid armored catfish and other fish with barbels, such as barbs, are especially liable to injure themselves when searching for food. Any wounds can easily become infected, and the fish may die as a result.

➤ In addition, the substrate should be lime free because calcium hardens the water and raises the pH.

➤ You may only use calcareous rocks if you are keeping fish that need an alkaline pH, such as cichlids from Lake Malawi or Lake Tanganyika. You can find out if a rock contains calcium by using the hydrochloric acid test.

➤ Particle size and substrate depth depend on the needs of the fish. Most aquariums use sand or gravel with a particle size of $^1/8$ inch (3–4 mm), which is added to a depth of about 2 inches (4–6 cm). If the substrate is too fine-grained, it often becomes clogged with debris and begins to decay. This can lead to the production of highly toxic hydrogen sulfide. If the substrate is too coarse-grained, bits of food can disappear into the spaces between the gravel, decay, and foul the water.

74. Substrate: I like the appearance of white gravel as a substrate. Can I use it in the aquarium?

It is better not to use a light-colored substrate because it reflects light, and this can irritate many fish and make them skittish. In most tropical waters, the substrate is dark. For this reason, a dark substrate is more like the natural environment of most fish. For the good of your fish, use dark gravel rather than white. This will also accentuate the colors of most fish, except for Mollies and a few other nearly black species.

75. Tank Material: The pet store carries aquariums made of various materials. Which material is the best?

The best choice is a glass tank. Glass aquariums are available in a variety of different shapes. There are manufacturing standards for adhesives and sealants as well as for the thickness of the aquarium glass, which vary according to the size of the tank and the water level. Most aquarium manufacturers follow these guidelines, so you can be relatively certain that the glass aquariums on the market are of good quality and the glass will withstand the water pressure.

If you want an especially large tank, you can also build one and equip it with a thick glass front.

Plastic aquariums are suitable for only small volumes of water up to 15 gallons (60 L). Besides, they are easily scratched, and that ruins the view. If you want to enjoy watching your fish for any length of time, buy a glass tank.

If you opt for a glass tank, just be sure to place it in a safe and sturdy location. This will ensure the protection of both your fish and your family members, especially if you live with a dog or cat.

76. Tank Shape: Aquariums are available in a variety of shapes. What should I keep in mind when choosing one?

Pet stores carry aquariums in many different shapes. The rectangular shape is the most common. This comes in standard sizes, for example 50 gallons (200 L) with sides measuring 30 inches × 18 inches × 18 inches (76 cm × 46 cm × 46 cm) or 15 gallons (60 L) measuring 24 inches × 12 inches × 12 inches (60 cm × 30 cm × 30 cm). These standard shapes have stood the test of time. For this reason, I suggest you buy a rectangular tank with a hood; you can then adjust your fish stock to fit the size of the tank. With these shapes, you can be certain that the ratio of water volume to water surface area will be correct. A good alternative to a rectangular tank is a corner aquarium. It looks very attractive in the corner of a room and also takes up less space.

Tanks are also available with unusual shapes, for instance pentagonal or hexagonal tanks. Aquariums like this are often placed in the center of a room as a special eye-catching feature. The disadvantage of this, of course, is that the electrical cords are out in the open and tripping over them is easy if they are not covered with carpets. Hoods are usually available for only rectangular tanks. Corner aquariums and six- or eight-sided tanks are usually left open and are illuminated by hanging lights. That has its disadvantages, too.

77. Tank Shape: Can I keep two Goldfish in a goldfish bowl?

You should never buy spherical aquariums like goldfish bowls, wall aquariums, or column aquariums. Fish cannot be kept properly in tanks like this, and using them is inhumane. There is not enough swimming room in these tanks, even for very small fish. In shallow wall aquariums, for example, the fish can barely turn around, much less retreat or hide, even if they are small species. Moreover, in oddly shaped tanks like this, the ratio of surface area to water volume is too low. The surface area of the water must be large so that enough oxygen can dissolve in the aquarium water. If the ratio is wrong, oxygen levels can easily drop too low. For the same reason, very tall, narrow tanks are not a good idea, either.

78. Tank Size: I would like to buy my first aquarium. How large should the tank be?

A reasonable size, especially for beginners, is an aquarium with a capacity of 25 gallons (100 L), although it can certainly be larger. A large tank is much easier to take care of than a small one because the water parameters are much more stable. For example, if the heater fails, a large tank holding 100 gallons (400 L) cools very slowly, while a small tank with just 15 gallons (60 L) cools in just a few hours. If you happen to be away from home when your tank cools down, your fish could die. The same holds true for other water parameters like pH, hardness, and oxygen level. If you make a mistake like accidentally dumping in too much food or failing to notice a dead fish, it will not have as dramatic an effect on the water quality in a large tank as it will in a small one. Aquariums smaller than 15 gallons (60 L) are not suitable for keeping fish for any length of time. For this reason, you should definitely avoid so-called desktop aquariums or minitanks. You should always provide a humane environment for your fish. Not only is this the right thing to do, but it will also mean your fish live longer and healthier lives.

79. Tank Size: Are there situations in which a small aquarium is a good idea?

Yes, sometimes a small aquarium is useful.

For instance, using only small tanks is customary at fish shows. Since show tanks usually hold just one fish or a small group, they normally have relatively small dimensions, especially for smaller fish like Guppies. They make it easier to observe and judge the fish. Since the fish are in them for only a short time, even a rather small tank is acceptable. Small tanks are also used in breeding. Only in rare cases is it possible to raise appreciable numbers of baby fish in a community tank. For this reason, many aquarists provide breeding tanks where their fish can spawn. Spawning often requires the creation of special conditions, which is no simple matter in a large aquarium or a community tank. Baby fish are usually raised in separate small tanks, as well, so that they can be fed according to their special needs, observed carefully, and protected from hungry predators.

80. Tank Volume: How do I calculate the capacity of my aquarium? Can I put as much water in my tank as I calculated?

Here is how to determine the maximum volume of your aquarium. Start by measuring the lengths of the sides in inches (cm). Multiply the length by the width and the height. Then divide the result by 250 (1,000). This gives you the number of gallons (liters) that will fit in the tank if it is filled to maximum capacity. For example: 40 inches (100 cm) long × 20 inches (50 cm) wide × 16 inches (40 cm) high = 12,800 (200,000). This number divided by 250 (1,000) is about 50 gallons (200 L). Theoretically, this aquarium could hold 50 gallons (200 L) of water. In practice, though, you would never fill an aquarium like this with 50 gallons (200 L) of water. You would always leave a little space between the water surface and the top of the tank. The decorations and the substrate also displace a considerable volume of water. For this reason, you have to subtract about 10–20 percent from the calculated volume, depending on the decorations and the water level, in order to find the actual volume of water in the tank. In the example, you would have to subtract about 5–10 gallons (20–40 L), which would give you an actual water volume of 40–45 gallons (160–180 L).

81. Tank Volume: Why is knowing the exact volume of a tank important?

There are several reasons why knowing how much water is in the aquarium is important. First of all, the volume of water available determines how many fish the tank can hold. In the second place, you need this number if you want to figure out the weight of the tank. One gallon of water weighs about 8 pounds (= 1 kg/L). Last but not least, the water volume plays a role when you have to administer medications since the amount you add depends on the volume of water in the tank. If you underdose because you do not know the exact volume, the effect of the medication can be reduced or lost entirely. An overdose, on the other hand, can harm the fish.

82. Transporting Plants: What is the best way to transport newly purchased aquarium plants?

When you bring newly purchased plants home from the store, you should make sure that they are not exposed to any extreme fluctuations in temperature. Most plants can be transported in plastic bags with a bit of water or while wrapped in wet newspapers.

83. **Types of Lighting: So many different kinds of lamps are available for lighting the aquarium. Which type is recommended?**

Which type of lighting is right for an aquarium depends on the size of the tank and the requirements of the fish and plants.

➤ Most freshwater aquariums are illuminated with fluorescent bulbs. They are available in a variety of color temperatures. You should figure on at least 2 watts of light per gallon (4 L) of aquarium water. Bulbs of different colors can also be combined with each other. In long tanks, the bulbs should be staggered in order to provide well-balanced illumination. Special plant bulbs with a high proportion of blue light (short-wavelength light) promote the growth of the plants. However, they should always be combined with bulbs producing longer wavelengths. You can use fluorescent bulbs for tanks up to 20 inches (50 cm) deep.

➤ You should use metal halide lamps (HQI) or mercury vapor lamps (HQL) to illuminate very large or deep aquariums. HQI lamps are very efficient and have good color rendition. They are somewhat better than HQL lamps and are the preferred choice.

EXTRA TIP

Attaching aquarium lamps
The simplest solution to the problem of how and where to attach the lamps for your fish and plants is to get an aquarium with a hood. The sockets for the fluorescent bulbs are already integrated in this hood. For open-topped aquariums, you have to attach pendant or hanging lamps to the ceiling at a suitable distance from the water surface. These lamps are equipped with HQI or HQL bulbs.

➤ Incandescent bulbs are unsuitable as a source of illumination. An incandescent bulb produces too little light and far too much heat. The color spectrum or wavelengths are not very well suited for an aquarium, either.

➤ Halogen (metal halide) lamps have a somewhat better light output than incandescent bulbs. They can be used as spotlights for special effects. However, they produce too little blue light for plant growth. They are not adequate as the only source of light for an aquarium.

84. Underwater Spotlights: I really like underwater spotlights in the aquarium. Are there any problems with using them?

Under natural conditions, the light always comes from above. If you use spotlights in your aquarium that shine on the fish from the side or from below, you may get some interesting effects. However, lighting like this is totally unnatural for the fish and will make it difficult for them to get their bearings. Since underwater spotlights are more likely to cause stress for your fish, you would do better to stay away from them and other novelties, like laser effects.

85. UV Lamps: Why do aquarists use UV lamps?

UV lamps are used to sterilize the water and are generally placed either before or after the filter. At the correct output, they will kill germs as the water flows past the UV source. A UV lamp lets you improve the water quality if your tank is affected by certain diseases, by turbidity due to unicellular algae, or has high bacterial levels. However, the use of a UV lamp is only a supportive measure. You still have to determine what is actually causing the proliferation of bacteria or algae and correct the problem.

86. Water Tests: What do I have to keep in mind when handling test reagents?

Test reagents are chemicals and, depending on the substance, can be harmful to humans. Because these chemicals are frequently irritating to the skin or even caustic, you have to make sure that they do not get onto your skin or clothing. If that happens, you must rinse them off thoroughly with water.

Never use a liquid test kit in the aquarium itself. Instead, always test a sample of the water in a separate container. Read the information on the bottles or packages carefully and follow the instructions.

To prevent the reagents from aging too quickly, the test kits should be stored in a cool, dark, dry place like the refrigerator. Be sure to label the test kits clearly and close them tightly. If children are in your home, though, the refrigerator is not the right storage place. Liquid test kits must always be kept out of reach of children.

In addition, the reagents have only a limited shelf life. Do not use them after the expiration date, or they can give you false results.

87. Wood: Can I use any kind of wood in my aquarium?

Pet stores carry a wide assortment of decorative wood that can be used for aquariums, for example, mopani wood, opuwa wood, bogwood, or mangrove roots. Since bogwood acidifies the water, you should use it only in aquariums containing fish that prefer soft and slightly acidic water. This is true of most fish native to the Amazon region. Bogwood can be used

Overleaf: Wood is a nice decoration in a tank, but make sure that you use a variety that is compatible with your fish.

with Discus; Angelfish; many characins like Head-and-taillight Tetras, Black Tetras, and Neon Tetras; as well as suckermouth armored catfish and callichthyid armored catfish.

Bogwood often releases tannins and pigments that are not really harmful but that stain the water yellow or brown. For this reason, I suggest that you soak the wood for a few days in a bucket of water in order to remove at least some of these unwanted substances.

You should not use bogwood if you are keeping fish that need hard and slightly alkaline water. This applies to fish from the East African rift lakes (Lakes Tanganyika and Malawi), for example, Africa Peacock Cichlids, Yellow Peacock Cichlids, Slender Cichlids, Malawi Blue Cichlids, or various shell-dwelling cichlids. A good alternative is to decorate the aquarium with mangrove roots or rocks from the pet store. You should be sure to soak mangrove roots for a while, too. When you do this, do not forget to change the water daily.

Never use roots that you find in your local woods. They will decay in the tank and foul the water. Theoretically, you could use wood that you find in swampy areas since these have been preserved in the swamp under anaerobic conditions and will no longer decay. Be careful! Many swamps are nature preserves and nothing can be removed from these areas.

EXTRA TIP

Boiling wood
In addition to soaking the wood, boiling it can be helpful. This removes much of the air from the wood, making it lose its buoyancy and stay on the bottom instead of floating at the water surface. To do this, put the wood into boiling water and boil it vigorously for five to ten minutes. Then let it dry out well before you put it into the aquarium.

Anatomy and Behavior

How do ornamental fish manage to survive in their environment and reproduce successfully? The following pages answer important questions about anatomy, physiology, coloration, and behavior.

88. Age: **Is determining the age of a fish possible from its scales?**

Yes, fish scales, just like trees, can have so-called growth rings. As a fish grows, the number of its scales does not increase; instead, the scales grow along with the fish. This annual increase in size can be determined from the rings.

Growth rings are found only in fish from temperate zones where there is an alternation between summer and winter. This is because growth stops during hibernation, leading to the formation of rings on the scales.

89. Age: **How long can fish live?**

It depends on the species. Many larger cichlids have an average life expectancy of 10–15 years. Killifish, which are also known as annual fish, are found in pools or ditches that are filled with water for only a brief period. Many killifish, even those kept in the aquarium under optimal conditions, live for barely more than a year. Most of the smaller aquarium fish, like Platies, Guppies, Tiger Barbs, or Neon Tetras, can live for several years. Catfish often reach an advanced age. One of my corydoras catfish even lived to be almost 20 years old.

In general, aquarium fish often live considerably longer than their relatives in the wild, a large percentage of which never even reach sexual maturity because they are killed by predators. Large fish species usually live longer than small, active fish. In principle, the life expectancy of fish from colder waters is greater than that of fish from the tropics.

Fish keeping, then, is a long-term commitment on the part of the pet owner. Before you create an aquarium, make sure that you will be able to care for your fish over the long haul.

LIFE EXPECTANCIES OF FISH

FISH SPECIES	SCIENTIFIC NAME	MAXIMUM AGE IN YEARS
Bristlenose Catfish	*Ancistrus* spp.	Up to 16
Discus	*Symphysodon aequifasciatus*	Up to 14
Firemouth Cichlid	*Thorichthys meeki*	Up to 15
Goldfish	*Carassius auratus giebelio*	30–40
Kissing Gourami	*Helostoma temminckii*	Up to 15
Neon Tetra	*Paracheirodon innesi*	Up to 7
Cory Catfish	*Corydoras* spp.	15 or more
Redchin Panchax	*Epiplatys dageti*	Up to 3
Swordtail, Platy, Guppy	*Xiphophorus hellerii, Xiphophorus maculatus, Poecilia reticulata*	Up to 4
Angelfish	*Pterophyllum scalare*	Up to 10
Siamese Fighting Fish	*Betta splendens*	Up to 3
Tiger Barb	*Puntius tetrazona*	Up to 5
Black Tetra	*Gymnocorymbus ternetzi*	Up to 3
Ram	*Mikrogeophagus ramirezi*	Up to 3
Zebra Danio	*Danio rerio*	Up to 3
Dwarf Gourami	*Colisa lalia*	Up to 4

90. Aggressive Behavior: **I had a school of Black Tetras. They all died except for one fish, which is now attacking all the other fish in the tank. What should I do to stop this?**

Black Tetras (*Gymnocorymbus ternetzi*) are schooling fish and need other members of their species in order to express their normal behavior. In the absence of others of their kind, they can develop behavioral problems like aggressiveness or extreme shyness. For this reason, you should either give the remaining fish to someone who already has a school of Black Tetras or buy at least four additional Black Tetras for your solitary fish.

91. Aggressive Behavior: **Do so-called Kissing Gouramis really kiss when they make contact with their mouth?**

No, it is just the opposite. When two fish grab onto each other with their mouths, this is an aggressive behavior. Rival males use their mouth to push and pull each other in order to establish which one is stronger. Many male killifish (*Aphyosemion* spp.) and dwarf cichlids (*Apistogramma* spp.) also fight in this manner. Since their lips are not as large those of the Kissing Gourami (*Helostoma temminckii*) or the Guyana Eye-spot Cichlid (*Heros* sp. Franz Guyana), it does not look like a kiss.

This aggressive behavior is called lip-locking or mouth wrestling. In the process, the combatants can injure each other severely before the final outcome of the contest is decided. Although the details of fighting behavior in cichlids differ from species to species, the basic features are similar.

You should monitor your fish to make certain that aggressive behavior does not turn into deadly behavior. If you think your fish may injure each other, you should separate them in different tanks.

92. Alarm Substances: **Can fish warn their companions of danger?**

Many fish, especially schooling fish like the Eurasian Minnow (*Phoxinus phoxinus*), secrete so-called alarm substances from glands in their skin when they are injured or stressed. Others members of their species can perceive these substances in the water, even in very low concentrations, and so are alerted to the presence of an enemy. The alarm substances immediately trigger a flight reaction, and other fish will continue to avoid this spot for quite a while.

93. Barbels: **My catfish have barbels around the mouth. What is the function of these barbels?**

Barbels are well supplied with taste receptors and could be described as a sort of external tongue. Fish use them to find and identify food as they

Which one is stronger? Mouth wrestling will decide.

feel around in the substrate. In addition, the barbels help fish form a three-dimensional image of their environment. Barbels are present primarily in bottom-dwelling and bottom-feeding fish.

The number of barbels can also be used in the systematic classification of fish. For example, although North American freshwater catfish have four pairs of barbels, European catfish have only three pairs.

94. Body Temperature: **Do fish maintain a constant body temperature the way we do?**

Most fish, like amphibians and reptiles, do not have a constant body temperature as birds and mammals do. Instead, they adopt the temperature of their environment. They are said to be cold-blooded (poikilothermic). That is why it is very important to keep your tank at the temperature required by your fish. Every fish species can tolerate fluctuations of a few degrees. However, if you go below this tolerance range, the fish will be chilled. They will then be less active and their immune system will be weakened, making them more susceptible to infections. If the temperature is consistently too high, the oxygen level of the water will drop, shortening the life expectancy of the fish. If the water temperature is far too high, the fish can asphyxiate.

95. Bottom Feeding: **My Goldfish keep picking up sand from the bottom and then spitting it again. What is the meaning of this?**

This behavior is completely normal in bottom-feeding species. The fish dig through the substrate searching for anything edible. When they discover a likely morsel, they pick up the substrate in the mouth, swallow the edible parts—small organisms or bits of plant matter—and then spit out the indigestible part. You can observe this behavior in many other cyprinids, for example the Tiger Barb (*Puntius tetrazona*) and the Rosy Barb (*Puntius conchonius*) as well as in callichthyid armored catfish like *Corydoras* spp.

96. **Bubble Nest: My betta is making a lot of bubbles at the water surface and seems to be guarding this foam constantly. What does this mean?**

Your fish has built what is referred to as a bubble nest. Some labyrinth fish like the Siamese Fighting Fish (*Betta splendens*), Paradise Fish (*Macropodus opercularis*), and Blue Gourami (*Trichogaster trichopterus*) as well as hoplo catfish (*Hoplosternum* spp.) construct these bubble nests at the water surface. They are composed of air and a special secretion produced by the fish. The fish spawn in these bubble nests, and the eggs develop there until

The eggs develop in the bubble nest until they hatch.

the fry hatch. The bubbles produced by the fish contain substances that help protect the eggs and embryos from attack by bacteria and fungi. This nest is usually guarded and tended by the male. He keeps it in good repair and retrieves any eggs that sink to the bottom, as well as fry later on, and returns them to the nest.

97. Coloration: **I am fascinated by the magnificent colors of my fish. What is responsible for these colors?**

Pigments deposited in the skin are one of the things responsible for coloration in fish. Depending on their type and distribution, they can make a fish appear black, red, or yellow. Another factor is the reflection of light by the scales, which produces an iridescent effect. The silvery sparkle of many fish is due to a specific substance (guanine) that is deposited in the skin in the form of tiny crystals. Most fish can even vary their color. They can make it lighter, darker, or change it completely. Pencilfish, for example, change

1 *When Angelfish swim among plants, their striped pattern makes them difficult to detect.*

2 *This perfectly camouflaged Frogmouth Catfish can barely be distinguished from its surroundings.*

color at night in order to be better camouflaged in the dark. Many males display particularly gorgeous colors during mating season in order to attract females who are ready to spawn.

The color of an aquarium fish can also indicate its condition. Color indicates whether, for example, it is ready to mate, stressed, aggressive, or sick.

Colors and markings often serve to deceive predators. Some fish have a so-called eyespot on the rear end of their body. Predatory fish prefer to seize their prey by the head. A fish disguised with eyespots will escape with its life if the predator grabs a bit of fin rather than its head. Eyespots like these are usually found in marine fish, for example the Copperband Butterflyfish (*Chelmon rostratus*).

98. Coloration: **In the pet store I saw an Indian Glassfish (*Parambassis lala*) with an unnatural-looking color. Can fish be colored artificially?**

Pet stores sometimes carry fish with neonlike or fluorescent colors, although you are familiar with these species as relatively ordinary fish. Such painted glassfish or disco fish have been artificially colored by methods like dye injection. Sometimes other species are artificially colored as well, for example Cory Catfish (*Corydoras* spp.).

Juvenile fish can be induced to take on the gorgeous colors of adults by the administration of male sex hormones. However, these artificially colored fish usually lose their color again within a few months, or they die relatively quickly. For humane reasons alone, please do not buy fish like these.

Carotenoids are often added to commercial foods in order to intensify the red color of fish. You may be familiar with this from the so-called salmon trout, which is actually a normal trout. Its flesh is colored

red by feeding it carotenoids so that it looks like salmon. Goldfish (*Carassius auratus auratus*) and Koi (*Cyprinus carpio*), in particular, are given foods containing carotenoids to make them a deeper shade of red. Doing so produces no harmful side effects for the fish.

99. **Courtship: My six corydoras catfish are normally quite peaceful. After a water change, however, I frequently notice a lot of commotion and they chase each other around the tank. Why?**

With some fish species, a water change stimulates the urge to mate. If your catfish become agitated after a water change, I suspect they are engaging in courtship behavior. The males are probably pursuing a female that is ready to spawn. After the eggs have been fertilized, the female swims up and down the tank looking for suitable places to attach them. She does this by carrying the eggs in a pocket formed by her pectoral fins. If you look closely, you may see the transparent eggs, about 1/16 inch (2 mm) in diameter, adhering to fine-leaved plants or the aquarium glass. The eggs are usually devoured in short order by other occupants of the aquarium if they are not transferred to a rearing tank immediately after the female deposits them.

100. **Distinguishing the Sexes: How can I tell if my fish are males or females?**

In many species of fish, distinguishing males and females based on outward appearance alone is not possible. The only exception is during spawning when the female develops a somewhat plumper belly due to the presence of eggs.

➤ In live-bearing toothcarps, the males have a gonopodium, which is a modified anal fin that functions as a copulatory organ. Since females do not have this organ, you can easily tell them apart. Pregnant females, on the other hand, have a dark blotch behind the anal fin called a gravid spot. This distinguishes them from immature males.

➤ In other species, sexually mature males have brighter colors and larger fins than the females at all times, or at least when spawning. For example, you can clearly recognize the male Veiltail Siamese Fighting Fish because of his striking fins. In general, you can identify male rainbowfish, killifish, and labyrinth fish by their splendid colors. In many cichlids, the males are distinctly larger and more colorful than the females.

1

*This male Slender Cichlid (*Pseudotropheus elongatus*) displays the characteristic egg spots on his anal fin.*

2

*The pregnant female Guppy (*Poecilia reticulata*) has a conspicuous gravid spot behind the anal fin.*

3

*In the Kribensis (*Pelvicachromis pulcher*), the females are more colorful and have a red belly spot.*

➤ In Angelfish, Discus, and some other cichlids, you can differentiate males and females during courtship by the form of the breeding tube. It is broad in females, while in males it is narrow and pointed.

➤ The Kribensis (*Pelvicachromis pulcher*), however, is an exception. In this species, the females are more colorful than the males. In addition, the females have a red belly spot.

➤ In many mouthbreeding cichlids, such as the Slender Cichlid (*Pseudotropheus elongatus*) or the Malawi Blue Cichlid (*Mettriaclima zebra*), the males have characteristic markings on the anal fin called egg spots.

➤ In cyprinids (barbs, danios, and rasboras), the males are often more colorful, and the females are plumper. For instance, the male Zebra Danio (*Danio rerio*) is usually yellowish while the female has whiter stripes.

101. Drinking: Do fish also need liquids, and can they drink?

Yes, fish do need liquids.

➤ Freshwater fish do not drink since they take in water through their gills and skin. Water enters on its own due to osmotic pressure because the fluid in the fish's cells contains more salts than the surrounding water. Water always flows from areas of low salt concentration to areas of high salt concentration in order to equalize the different concentrations. Freshwater fish excrete the excess water through their kidneys. If they did not do that, the cells of their body would burst due to the continual uptake of water.

➤ In saltwater fish, the reverse is true. The salt concentration in sea water is considerably higher than in the body of the fish. Consequently, the salt water draws the water out of the fish's body. Marine fish drink through the mouth and the gills, but they do not absorb water through the skin. Special mechanisms in the gills prevent salt from entering, so only demineralized water is allowed into the body.

102. Fins: **What is meant by paired and unpaired fins?**

The appearance of a fish is determined by its fins. In principle, there are two types of fins: paired and unpaired. Paired means that the same type of fin is found on both the left and right sides of the body. Pelvic and pectoral fins are always paired. Caudal, anal, and dorsal fins are usually unpaired, which means there is only one of each. Some species, like many characins or catfish, also have an additional fin called the adipose fin.

103. Fins: **What are the different types of fins in fish, and what are their functions?**

➤ The fish uses its dorsal and anal fins to maintain balance and direction when swimming. The pectoral fins are used to swim upward or downward, to brake, and for stability. The pelvic fins are also involved in braking; a fish spreads them out to keep from sinking.

INFO

The adipose fin
Many characins, such as the Lemon Tetra (*Hyphessobrycon pulchripinnis*), and catfish, like the Bronze Corydoras (*Corydoras aeneus*), have what is called an adipose fin behind the dorsal fin. It consists primarily of fatty tissue and differs from the other fins by the absence of fin rays. Its function is unknown.

➤ In addition to assisting in locomotion, fins also perform other functions. The female Cory Catfish (*Corydoras* spp.) can use her pelvic fins to make a sort of pocket. During spawning, she uses this to catch her eggs and carry them to a suitable spot where she can adhere them. Some bottom-dwelling fish use their pectoral fins to support themselves on the substrate. Other fish can even move on land with the aid of their fins. In many fish, for instance bettas, the fins also play an important role in courtship when the fish spread their impressive fins in an attempt to intimidate their rivals.

➤ Sometimes the fins have been modified so that they can take on special functions. In all live-bearing toothcarps, for instance, the anal fin of the male has been transformed into a copulatory organ called the gonopodium.

➤ In some gobies that live in fast-flowing streams, the pelvic fins have developed into sucking or adhesive disks. They function like a suction cup, and the fish can use them to hold tight in a strong current. Gouramis use their long pectoral fins, which bear touch and taste receptors, to examine their surroundings and to search for food.

104. Flying Fish: **Are there really fish that can fly?**

Yes, some marine saltwater fish like flyingfish (family Exocoetidae) have this ability. They have greatly enlarged pectoral fins that they can use to glide through the air for relatively long distances (up to 200 yards/200 m). However, some freshwater fish can also travel over the water by leaping. They exhibit this behavior especially when frightened or pursued by predatory fish. Leaping out of the water often saves the life of the quarry. In the aquarium, however, this behavior can lead to disaster if the tank is open. Marbled Hatchetfish (*Carnegiella strigata*) are among the best jumpers. If you keep these fish, you should be sure to cover the tank and leave at least 4 inches (10 cm) between the tank cover and the water surface so that the fish do not hurt themselves on the cover glass.

105. Hearing: **Can fish hear, and does loud music disturb them?**

In principle, all fish can hear and react to noises. However, the ability to hear is developed to different degrees depending on the species of fish. Fish, like mammals, have a so-called inner ear with which they can perceive sounds. Some fish, for example characins, can transmit sound waves from the swim bladder to the inner ear by means of tiny bones called Weberian ossicles. Their ability to hear is especially good.

Regardless of the species in your aquarium, you should not forget that water has a higher density than air. This means that sounds are transmitted much better underwater than on land. Consequently, loud music sounds even louder to fish, and they probably find it stressful.

106. Lateral Line Organ: **Why do my fish not collide with the glass wall of the aquarium or bump into each other when they are swimming in a school?**

This is prevented by a structure called the lateral line organ, which the fish use as a sort of remote sensing device. In most fish, this organ runs along the middle of the body in a slightly curved line from the head to the base of the tail. It is composed of lateral line canals that are filled with liquid and supplied with sensory cells. These, in turn, communicate directly with the surrounding water by means of pores, which are tiny holes in the scales. Even small changes in water currents are registered and reported to the brain by nerves. This way, fish can perceive the slightest pressure waves in the water, such as those produced by other fish. As a result, they avoid colliding with these fish or are warned of potential predators. Fish also use this organ to detect waves reflected by objects like rocks or the glass wall of the aquarium.

107. Learning Ability: **Can fish actually learn?**

Yes, fish can learn. You can test this quite easily yourself. If you feed your fish at the same place and the same time every day, they will soon learn where and when they will find food and will swim expectantly to this spot at mealtime. Some fish are also quick to realize that they get food from their owner's hand. This ability to learn is especially pronounced in cichlids and Koi.

The lateral line organ helps fish get their bearings.

108. Live Birth: **Are there fish who give birth to live young?**

Among the fish that give birth to live young are half-beaks, splitfins, and live-bearing toothcarps. This last group includes Guppies (*Poecilia reticulata*), Platies (*Xiphophorus maculatus*), Mollies (*Poecilia sphenops* var.), and Swordtails (*Xiphophorus hellerii*). Of course, the development of the young inside the mother's body cannot be compared with fetal development in mammals. In live-bearing toothcarps, the eggs develop into baby fish inside the mother, and then at birth the shells split open, releasing the baby fish (called fry). There is no placenta or umbilical cord like that found in mammals, although splitfins have something like an umbilical cord connecting the embryos and the maternal tissue.

109. Organs: **Do fish have the same internal organs as mammals?**

Many of the organs familiar to you from mammals are also found in fish. To some extent, though, they function differently than in mammals. In both fish and mammals, the heart pumps blood through the

EXTRA TIP

Live-bearing fish
Live birth has its advantages. By the time the fry are born, they have already reached an advanced stage of development and so are less likely to be devoured by predators. Immediately after birth, they can look for hiding places, perhaps among plants, where they can be sheltered as they grow up. If you have an aquarium with live-bearers, plant it densely if you want the young to survive, and do not keep predatory fish like Angelfish in the same tank.

circulatory system, and the liver is used for storage and metabolism. The kidneys, which lie directly below the backbone, produce urine as in mammals, but they are also responsible for blood formation, a function performed in mammals by the bone marrow. Fish, like mammals, also have a digestive tract with a stomach—although this is present only in predatory fish—and an intestine. In plant-eating species, the digestive tract is very long. Female fish have ovaries, and males have testes. Fish do not have lungs since they breathe by means of gills. Only the lungfish, which are seldom kept by aquarists, have a lunglike organ.

110. Parental Care: What is meant by parental care in aquarium fish?

Parental care includes all the measures that fish use to protect their offspring, both eggs as well as newly hatched young, called fry. These include the parents' painstaking search for an appropriate spawning site, construction of the nest, and guarding of the eggs. The parents also remove unfertilized or moldy eggs and make sure the eggs get enough oxygen by fanning them with their fins. Fish use a variety of additional behaviors to ensure the survival of their offspring.

Depending on whether only the male, only the female, or both parents care for the offspring, fish are referred to as having patriarchal, matriarchal, or parental families.

111. Parental Care: Which fish display unusual types of parental care behavior?

Many fish species care for their offspring in very different ways.

➤ In bristlenose catfish (*Ancistrus* spp.), for example, males guard and care for the eggs. Even after hatching, the young remain near the father and escape into his cave at the first sign of danger.

➤ Male bettas build bubble nests in which the females lay their eggs. The male then guards the eggs. If the newly hatched fry get too far from the nest, the father picks them up in his mouth and carries them back to the nest.

➤ Parental behavior of the Cuckoo Catfish (*Synodontis multipunctatus*) is especially interesting. This fish, referred to as a brood parasite, slips her own eggs in among those of spawning cichlids.

➤ The type of parental care exhibited by the so-called mouthbreeders is remarkable. In these fish, the fry grow up in the mouth of the adult. This can happen in a variety of ways, depending on the species. In one type, the female lays her eggs on a substrate, where they are fertilized by the male. The eggs are guarded carefully until they hatch. Then one of the parents picks up the fry in its mouth. Whether the father or the mother does this varies from species to species. Other female mouthbreeders carry the unfertilized eggs in their mouth, where they are subsequently fertilized. Still other mouthbreeding species gather the eggs in their mouth after fertilization.

➤ The most highly developed type of parental care is displayed by splitfins (also known as goodeids). Here the fry develop inside the mother's body and are even nourished by a sort of umbilical cord. Parental care, however, ceases after birth.

112. Parental Care: My Angelfish spawned and then a few hours later they ate the eggs. What is the reason for this?

For one thing, this sort of behavior sometimes occurs with first-time parents. If your Angelfish devour the eggs of their next brood, too, you should first check the aquarium conditions.

A lot of commotion around the aquarium can cause the fish so much stress that they will eat their eggs or the newly hatched fry. At night you should leave a dim light burning so that the parent fish can get their bearings. Make sure that the water parameters in the tank are optimal. If you are certain that the environmental conditions are in order yet the fish continue to exhibit this undesirable behavior, replacing one of the partners sometimes helps. You can also remove the eggs and raise the young separately in a rearing tank.

If the parent fish are kept in a separate spawning tank, another reason for egg eating can be that the fish are unable to exhibit their territorial behavior because appropriate key stimuli, such as the presence of other fish, are absent. If you add two or three harmless dither fish like Swordtails, the behavior often changes abruptly. Now the parents should take exemplary care of their eggs and be very careful not to let the other fish get too close.

Whatever the cause of egg eating, you should take steps to prevent it.

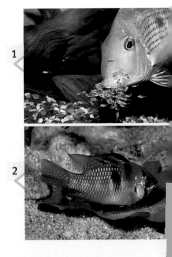

Interesting breeding behavior. In mouthbreeders, the fry grow up in the mouth of the father or mother.

1

This female Ram (Mikrogeophagus ramirezi) has laid her eggs on a leaf.

2

Unfortunately, the reason many Angelfish have poor parenting skills is that fry are reared in large breeding tanks without parents. Thus there is no selection for intact parental care, which is a genetically determined behavior.

113. Rearing Baby Fish: **Some fish in my aquarium had offspring, and I succeeded in raising them. What do I do with these young fish now?**

There are a variety of options for finding a good home for your juveniles. You can place an ad in your local paper or post a notice on the bulletin board at school. You can also contact an aquarium club in your neighborhood and ask when the next fish exchange will take place. There are even web sites on the Internet where you can sell your fish. Many pet dealers do not accept fish from private individuals unless they can provide large numbers or a regular supply of captive-bred fish. Most pet dealers get their fish from one supplier, usually a wholesaler, because of the danger of introducing disease. However, some independent stores are happy to get fish from breeders. You will just have to ask your local store.

INFO

How parents and young communicate
In order to protect their young, parent fish have developed specific signals and behaviors. A characteristic twitch of the fins, in which the pelvic, dorsal, and anal fins are suddenly erected and then folded back again, invites the young to gather around the parent. Female mouthbreeders tip downward and then bob up and down when they want to pick up the young in their mouth. The fry respond to this signal.

114. Reproduction: **How do fish reproduce?**

Fish have evolved various methods for reproduction. In most fish, the female deposits her eggs (called spawn or roe), which are then fertilized by the male. He does this by releasing sperm (also known as milt) over the eggs. However, in some fish like live-bearing toothcarps, fertilization occurs internally, within the female's body. The young develop in eggs inside the mother and are born live.

115. Reproduction: **I would like to have baby fish. How can I get my fish to spawn?**

That depends on the species of fish. Some species, like Guppies (*Poecilia reticulata*), reproduce readily, while other species will not spawn without special tricks.

The best thing to do is find some information on the species that you would like to breed. Aquarists who have already bred this species can also give you advice.

Most species normally will not produce offspring in a community tank. Instead, they need a separate breeding tank. Some fish, like the Cory Catfish (*Corydoras* spp.), will be stimulated to lay eggs by a water change. Other fish require a specific spawning substrate or fine-leaved plants in order to lay their eggs. Feeding live mosquito larvae is supposed to stimulate spawning in almost all aquarium fish.

Many of the live-bearing toothcarps are the easiest fish to breed. They reproduce in the community tank, and their young can be raised easily if no predatory fish are in the tank. Egg-laying fish that are relatively easy to breed include the Zebra Danio (*Danio rerio*), White Cloud Mountain Minnow (*Tanichthys albonubes*), and Paradise Fish (*Macropodus opercularis*).

However, these fish require a species tank or a separate breeding tank.

Starlight Bristlenose Catfish (*Ancistrus dolichopterus*) also reproduce in the community tank if you give them a cave where the female can lay her eggs. These are then tended by the male.

116. Reproduction: **I discovered some baby fish in my aquarium. What can I do to raise them?**

If they are Guppies (*Poecilia reticulata*) or other live-bearing toothcarps and no predatory fish are in your tank, you can leave the babies in the same tank, provided you have enough room in there for more fish. If you overcrowd, you will soon have problems with the water quality. In any case, you should provide plenty of hiding places, for example, floating plants, Java Moss, or carved rock.

If larger fish are in the tank that could pose a danger to the babies, you should remove the tiny fish carefully, perhaps using a drinking glass. Important— It is imperative that the sensitive babies remain under water. Put them into a small rearing tank—about 5–10 gallons (25–45 L)—and no substrate.

INFO

Brood parasites in the aquarium
In the Cuckoo Catfish (*Synodontis multipunctatus*), nature has come up with something special. The catfish parents look for foster mothers for their offspring. When catfish are ready to spawn, they find some spawning mouthbreeding cichlids. Just when the female cichlid has laid her eggs and is gathering them up in her mouth to care for the brood, the catfish deposit their own eggs among those of the cichlid. The catfish eggs then hatch in the cichlid's mouth.

This makes it easier to suction up leftover food with a thin hose. A small air-driven internal filter and an aquarium water heater complete the setup. You can also add some Java Moss to provide hiding places for the babies. You must use aquarium water from the original tank since the babies are very sensitive to changes in water quality.

117. Respiration: How does gill respiration work?

Instead of lungs, fish have a different respiratory organ: the gills. These are located on both sides of the head behind the eyes and are protected by gill covers, or opercula. The gills are richly supplied with blood vessels. Therefore under normal conditions, they are bright red in color.

Gill respiration works as follows. The water enters through the mouth, is channeled through the gills, and then flows out again through the raised gill covers. In the process, each gill filament is constantly bathed by fresh respiratory water so that oxygen can be absorbed directly from the water and carbon dioxide can be given off into it. You can easily see the regular movements of the gill covers during respiration when you watch your fish.

118. Respiration: Do aquarium fish have other methods besides gill respiration for taking in oxygen?

A few fish have developed supplementary methods of respiration, especially if the water in their natural habitat is very poorly oxygenated.

➤ Many catfish, for example callichthyid armored catfish like *Corydoras* spp., use supplemental intestinal respiration. They gulp in air at the surface of the water and then absorb oxygen from this air through the intestinal mucosa.

➤ Labyrinth fish have an accessory structure in the head called the labyrinth organ that allows them to take in atmospheric oxygen. That is why fish with labyrinth organs—which include bettas, paradise fish, and gouramis—must always have access to the water surface. Because of the labyrinth organ, these fish can even live in habitats where there is often a lack of oxygen, for instance in muddy, stagnant, or very warm water.

➤ Lungfish, which are seldom kept in aquariums, have a lunglike organ that helps them take in oxygen from the air.

➤ A type of skin breathing is also possible in young fish and fry. They can absorb oxygen directly from the water through their skin.

119. Sensitivity to Pain: **Can my fish feel pain?**

Even if many fishermen would like to argue the point, scientists have demonstrated that fish are sensitive to stress and pain. They react to pain stimuli and also have the neural pathways necessary for pain perception.

Since fish cannot cry out, they suffer in silence. However, they do show changes in behavior like loss of color, fin clamping, and rapid breathing. That is why you should watch your fish carefully so that you will notice right away if something is wrong.

If you believe that your fish are in pain, you should consult a veterinarian immediately. He or she should be able to tell you the cause of the problem and how to get rid of it. The problem may lie in the quality of the aquarium water or it might be disease. In any case, you should not let your fish suffer in pain.

120. Sight: Can fish see well?

Most fish can see quite well. They have what are referred to as lens eyes. In order to see something in sharp focus, fish can use special muscles to push the lens in or out, depending on how far away the object is. In humans and other mammals, this is done by changing the curvature of the lens. Fish have depth perception in the visual field in front of the head where the visual angles of the two eyes overlap. They also perceive movement very well. This is especially important when searching for food, finding their way, and detecting enemies.

Fish can see colors, too. This is apparent because in many fish, color plays an important role in communication among members of the species. For instance during courtship, males are often much more colorful than the females. A look at the anatomy of the eyes also reveals the presence of all structures necessary for color perception. In the Blind Cave Fish, a colorless variety of the Mexican Tetra (*Astyanax mexicanus*) that lives in complete darkness, the eyes are rudimentary, and consequently the fish is blind.

121. Slime Coat: Why do many fish feel so slippery to the touch?

Glands in the skin of the fish produce mucus that coats the entire body. This slime has a variety of functions. For one thing, it has antimicrobial properties and protects the fish from bacterial and fungal infections. If the slime coat is damaged, a skin infection can quickly follow. To avoid damaging the slime coat, you should never touch your fish with dry, bare hands.

In addition, the slippery slime coat provides some protection against capture by predators. It also reduces resistance as the fish moves through the water.

122. Sound Production: **I have an aquarium in my bedroom with Guppies, Zebra Danios, and dwarf armored catfish. I keep hearing croaking sounds, especially at night. Are these coming from the fish?**

Yes, fish can indeed make noise. Scientists have shown that some fish can produce a variety of sounds, usually by rubbing skeletal elements against each other. The fish use these sounds to communicate with each other, especially when defending their territory and during courtship. The croaking that you hear at night probably comes from the male catfish, who are fighting over territory.

123. Stomach: **Is it true that some fish do not have a stomach?**

Yes; cyprinids, in particular, do not have a stomach. These include the egg-laying and live-bearing toothcarps as well as barbs, danios, and rasboras. Instead, the intestine is much longer and assumes the function of the stomach. Food is digested here, and the nutrients can be absorbed through the intestinal mucosa. In contrast, predatory fish like cichlids almost all have a stomach where food undergoes the initial stages of digestion before it arrives at the intestines.

124. Stress: **Can my fish experience stress? If so, how can I tell?**

Fish can feel stress. It reduces their resistance to disease and makes them more susceptible to illness. Stress can be caused by a dominant fish that chases subordinate fish around the aquarium. These subordinate fish have to stay hidden and may not get enough to eat. Overcrowding, transport, or a new environment can likewise lead to stress. With many species, you can tell if the fish are stressed by their coloration. Although they were bright and colorful in the dealer's tank, they look pale and transparent in the plastic bag on the way home. Only after they have acclimated do the fish again display their colors in their original beauty.

125. **Swim Bladder: I sometimes have the impression that my fish are not swimming in the water but instead are actually floating. Why is that?**

Fish are the only creatures that have a swim bladder. This unusual organ originated as a gas-filled out-pouching of the digestive tract. The swim bladder allows a fish to swim at whatever depth it wants. The fish can regulate the amount of gas in the swim bladder and so can adjust its buoyancy to suit the water pressure, which varies according to the depth of the water. This way the fish actually achieves a sort of weightless state and has to expend less energy when swimming.

By the way, not all fish have a swim bladder. It is absent, for instance, in cartilaginous fish like sharks, skates, and rays. However, these fish have a lot of fat in their liver, which gives them a certain amount of buoyancy. Some bony fish, like the Peacock Blenny (*Salaria pavo*), as well as species that are primarily bottom dwellers have no swim bladder, either.

126. **Taming: Can fish be tamed?**

Some fish actually can become tame. In garden ponds, Koi (*Cyprinus carpio*), in particular, are often quick to learn that humans will give them food. A few individuals even become so tame that they will let themselves be petted. In the aquarium, larger cichlids like the Oscar (*Astronotus ocellatus*) soon get to know their keepers and then eagerly accept extra helpings of food offered by hand or with tweezers. Schooling fish, on the other hand, almost never develop a relationship with their keepers. With many fish, you are making great progress if they no longer swim away in panic as soon as you approach the aquarium.

127. Taste: How do fish perceive taste?

The entire surface of the fish's body is covered with special sensory cells called taste buds. These are most numerous in and around the mouth. If the fish have barbels, the greatest number of taste buds are located there. Some labyrinth fish also have taste buds on the ends of their filamentous fin rays, which they use to investigate potential food items. Fish, like humans, can distinguish sweet, sour, salty, and bitter, but their ability to perceive taste is considerably more sensitive than ours. They can recognize flavored compounds even in very low concentrations.

EXTRA TIP

Feeding fry
For baby fish (fry) with a body length of 3/16 inch (4–5 mm) or more, you can use standard powdered fish food. Smaller fry must be fed infusoria or brine shrimp several times a day. Feeding your fry excessive amounts of food will quickly overload the water with organic wastes. Monitor the water parameters carefully, and carry out partial water changes every two to four days if necessary.

128. Territorial Behavior: **My two Red-tailed Black Sharks are always chasing each other around the tank. The smaller fish has even been injured. What can I do?**

Red-tailed Black Sharks (*Epalzeorhynchos bicolor*) are loners. No matter how large the aquarium, each fish regards the entire tank as its territory and will try to chase off other Redtails of either sex—except during the mating period. Since the subordinate fish cannot escape as it could in the wild, it is sometimes injured so severely that it dies. Therefore you should separate the fish as quickly as possible. If you cannot transfer one of the two Redtails to a second tank, you will have to give away one fish. In the future, before you buy fish, be sure to find out which species are loners, which you can keep in a community tank without difficulty, and which are schooling fish.

129. Urine Excretion: **Do fish excrete urine, and what happens to it in the water?**

Fish do excrete urine. The kidneys and ureters release the urine into the water. Toxic metabolic products like ammonia are also excreted into the water through the gills. In order to maintain an aquarium, you must understand these processes. They are the reason that you have to carry out regular water changes.

If your fish display territorial behavior, you will have to take steps to separate them. To avoid this problem in the first place, you should investigate which fish are likely to show this behavior before you populate your tank.

Fish and Their Communities

There are countless species of
fish. However, what do they need?
Which ones are compatible? This
chapter answers question about
the requirements of different
species, the right way to group
them into communities, and
suitable types of aquariums.

130. Amazon Tank: What is meant by an Amazon tank?

An Amazon tank is intended to represent a miniature version of life in the Amazon River and its tributaries. In a tank like this, use only fish that are native to the Amazon region, for instance various characins, cichlids like Angelfish and Discus, as well as callichthyid and suckermouth armored catfish.

131. Amazon Tank: I would like to set up an Amazon tank with a capacity of 65 gallons (250 liters). Which fish are suitable, and what must I keep in mind when setting it up?

A large tank with a capacity of 65 gallons (250 liters) provides enough space for eight to ten Panda Corys (*Corydoras panda*), one pair of bristlenose catfish (*Ancistrus* spp.), three pairs of Angelfish (*Pterophyllum scalare*), one male and two to four female Red-lined Dwarf Cichlids

The Amazon tank, nature in miniature.

(*Apistogramma hongsloi*), and one pair of Bolivian Rams (*Mikrogeophagus altispinosus*).

Make sure that the water for these fish is rather soft (up to 12°dGH) and neutral to slightly acidic (pH below 7). The water temperature should be between 77 and 82°F (25 and 28°C).

Most fish species from the Amazon benefit from peat filtration but only if your tap water is not too soft. Peat contains humic acids, which have a positive influence on the water quality. Adding peat to the filter lowers the pH and reduces the total hardness in the aquarium. The plants for your aquarium should also be indigenous to the Amazon region. Suitable plants are Brazilian Milfoil (*Myriophyllum aquaticum*), Brazilian Pennywort (*Hydrocotyle leucocephala*), pondweeds (*Potamogeton gayii*), and of course various species of swordplant (*Echinodorus* sp.). When planting, make sure to put the lower-growing species in the foreground and the taller ones in the background of the aquarium so that the fish have enough free swimming room and you can watch them easily.

Place a large piece of bogwood into the aquarium. It is very decorative, provides hiding places for the fish, and serves as a source of cellulose for the bristlenose catfish.

132. **Biotope Aquarium: I have read that aquarium fish should be kept in a natural environment. What does that mean in practice?**

If you would like your fish to have the most natural habitat possible, then you can provide it in what is referred to as a biotope aquarium. Basically, this is a tank in which you keep only fish and plants from a specific geographic region. For instance, an Amazon tank holds only fish and aquatic plants from the Amazon region. As far as decorations are concerned, you would only use materials occurring naturally in the Amazon.

Before buying a species, you should find out as much as possible about its origin and habitat conditions. For species that need hiding places, you have to provide suitable options, such as driftwood or artificial caves. Very active swimmers like the Giant Danio (*Danio aequipinnatus*) require swimming space that is free of plants or decorations. Some species, for example Siamese Fighting Fish (*Betta splendens*), need floating plants in order to build their bubble nests at the water surface.

133. Brackish-water Fish: What exactly are brackish-water fish?

Brackish-water fish live in the estuaries of rivers where freshwater mixes with seawater. The salinity of brackish water varies according to the season as well as in relation to the ebb and flow of the tide. The water temperature, oxygen level, and turbidity fluctuate as well. If brackish-water fish are kept in just freshwater, they usually do not live very long. That is why adding saltwater supplements to your tank is necessary if you keep these fish.

Among the brackish-water fish that you will frequently find in pet stores are the scats from Southeast Asia and Australia (e.g., *Scatophagus* spp.); glassfish (e.g., *Chanda ranga,* now known as *Parambassis ranga*); fingerfish or monos from Asia, Africa, and Australia (e.g., *Monodactylus argenteus*); sea catfish, also known as shark catfish (e.g., *Ariopsis seemanni*); archerfish (like *Toxotes* spp.); as well as many species of pufferfish (*Tetraodon* spp.).

If you are new to the fish-keeping hobby, you may want to start with either a freshwater or a saltwater aquarium. Maintaining the proper water parameters in a brackish-water aquarium can be tricky, and so is better left to an experienced aquarist.

134. Bristlenose Catfish: Is it true that bristlenose catfish need a piece of driftwood in the aquarium?

A piece of wood is always a good thing to have in the aquarium. Bristlenose catfish need generous amounts of cellulose, which is found in plants. If you do not feed your fish any vegetable matter, like slices of cucumber or potato, or suitable tablet foods, they can satisfy their requirement for cellulose by rasping away at the driftwood.

135. Catfish: What characterizes catfish?

Catfish include more than 3,000 species and are found throughout the world in temperate, subtropical, and tropical zones. They inhabit waters of all types. Most catfish are bottom dwellers and prefer to stay hidden. Many are crepuscular (active at dawn and dusk) and nocturnal (active at night). Their feeding preferences run all the way from plant- or algae-eating species to predators. South American callichthyid armored catfish eat small insect larvae and worms. Suckermouth armored catfish, which also come from South America, rasp off algae or small

INFO

Unusual catfish
In some species of catfish like the Croaking Spiny Catfish (*Ambyldoras hancocki*), the first rays of the pectoral fins and often the first ray of the dorsal fin are modified to form spinelike structures. These fish can spread their fins in such a way that predatory fish find swallowing them difficult or impossible. If you want to catch a catfish like this, use a very fine-meshed net; otherwise the fish will get entangled in the net and have to be cut out.

SOUTHEAST ASIA TANK

When setting up and aquascaping your aquarium, use nature as your guide. A Southeast Asia tank, for example, can reflect a little of the habitat of Southeast Asian fish, like a fast-flowing

HARLEQUIN RASBORAS

The species pictured on these two pages all have the same habitat requirements and can be kept together in a Southeast

Asia community tank. The lively Harlequin Rasboras (*Trigonostigma heteromorpha*) grow to be about 1¾ inches (4.5 cm) long and are happy only in a school.

CHINESE ALGAE-EATER

In the wild, Chinese Algae-Eaters (*Gyrinocheilus aymonieri*) inhabit rocky areas in fast-flowing streams. They feed

primarily on algae growing on rocks or on pieces of wood. Chinese Algae-Eaters can reach a length of 10 inches (25 cm) when fully grown and should be kept only in large tanks.

ROSY BARBS

The robust Rosy Barbs (*Puntius conchonius*) swim in small groups as they dig around in the substrate hunting for micro-

scopic prey. These fish, which grow to be about 4¾ inches (12 cm) long, often inhabit muddy waters in their native Southeast Asia. Here the barbel in the corners of their mouth help them to search for food.

stream with a fine-gravel bottom, rounded rocks covered with algae, driftwood, and long-leaved plants.

PEARL DANIOS
In the wild, they live in clear streams of the hill country where they prey on small insects that land on the water surface.

Pearl Danios (*Danio albolineatus*) grow to be about 2 ½ inches (6 cm) long and are agile schooling fish. Long tanks with zones of strong current are best for these lively fish.

CHERRY BARBS
This shy barb, which gets to be about 2 inches (5 cm) long, prefers to live in groups. Without others of its kind, it will pine

away. Cherry Barbs (*Puntius tittya*) should always be kept in a school of at least eight fish. They live near the bottom, where they search for microscopic foods like bits of plant matter and microorganisms.

TIGER BARBS
These robust schooling fish, which reach 2¾ inches (7 cm) in length, are one of the most popular species of barbs. Some-

times the males establish small territories, which they will defend against other barbs as well as other bottom-dwelling fish. Tiger Barbs (*Puntius tetrazona*) like to nip at the fins of other fish, especially long-finned species.

animals with their toothed suckerlike mouth. Species like the Dwarf Corys and Glass Catfish live among plants in the open water of quiet streams and eat water fleas and other microorganisms. A few species, like the Starlight Bristlenose Catfish, exhibit parental care, while others cease to tend their eggs after they have laid them. Full-grown catfish can grow to be anywhere from barely ¾ inch (2 cm) up to 10 feet (3 m) in length, depending on the species. They also differ greatly in shape.

Catfish have no scales on the surface of their body. In many species, the body is covered by bony plates, which protect it like a suit of armor. In addition, most species have barbels around the mouth that function as organs of taste and touch in feeding. Some catfish species, for example callichthyid armored catfish, have an unusual way of breathing. In addition to gill respiration, they can swallow atmospheric air and then absorb oxygen from it through the intestinal mucosa.

136. Catfish: What must I take into consideration if I want to keep catfish in the aquarium? ?

Most catfish kept in aquariums come from the following families: callichthyid armored catfish (*Corydoras* spp., *Brochis* spp., *Callichthys* spp., *Hoplosternum* spp.), North American freshwater catfish (*Ictalurus* spp.), suckermouth armored catfish (*Otocinclus* spp., *Hypostomus* spp., *Panaque* spp., *Rineloricaria* spp., *Ancistrus* spp.), and upside-down catfish (*Synodontis* spp.). A large number of catfish are bottom dwellers and so are ideally suited for keeping with fish that swim in the upper and middle water levels of a community aquarium. In addition, they get rid of any uneaten food that sinks to the bottom of the tank. This does not mean, though, that catfish do not need to be fed. After you switch off the lights, put some food tablets into the water to make sure the catfish get an adequate diet. Most catfish appreciate the company of others of their kind. This is absolutely necessary for Corys Catfish (*Corydoras* spp.). You should keep at least four individuals of a species in the aquarium. Since most catfish prefer subdued light, you can provide shady spots by using floating plants and some densely planted areas. Be sure to give them retreats and hiding places, as well, such as pieces of driftwood.

Some catfish, such as bristlenose catfish (*Ancistrus* spp.) and dwarf suckermouth catfish (*Otocinclus* spp.), like to eat algae.

137. Characins: Which fish belong to the characin family, and what characterizes them?

Characins (order Chariciformes), which include about 1,400 species, are found in Central and South America as well as in Africa. They live in both stagnant and running waters.

Most characins are schooling fish and need to be kept in groups of six to ten of the same species in order to be happy. There are about 45 genera with more than 50 species each.

A characteristic feature of characins is the adipose fin, which is located between the dorsal and caudal fins. However, not all species of characins have an adipose fin. Individual species can vary greatly in appearance. The small, blue-and-red-striped Cardinal Tetras

> *The Black Tetra is a popular aquarium fish. It belongs to the same group as hatchetfish.*

(*Paracheirodon axelrodi*) are characins, as are piranhas that grow up to 15 inches (38 cm) long. Other familiar representatives of this family are the Rummynose Tetra (*Hemigrammus bleheri*), the Ornate Tetra (*Hyphessobrycon bentosi*), the Congo Tetra (*Phenacogrammus interruptus*), and the Black Tetra (*Gymnocorymbus ternetzi*).

The feeding preferences of characins run the gamut from pure herbivores (rare) to carnivores (more common). In the aquarium, you can usually give them dry food with no problem. At least once a week, you should supplement their diet with live or frozen foods.

The vast majority of characins need soft, slightly acidic to neutral water. To make sure enough room is available for swimming, do not plant the aquarium too heavily. Since many characins are predatory, you should not keep them together with much smaller fish.

138. Cichlids: Which fish are known as cichlids?

Cichlids are members of the family Cichlidae; with more than 1,000 species, this is one of the largest families of freshwater fish. Chichlids have an undivided dorsal fin with both spiny rays and soft rays. Their range of distribution extends across Central and South America, Africa, southern India, and Sri Lanka.

Because of their attractive coloration and variety of shapes, and especially because of their interesting behavior, cichlids are very popular aquarium fish. The species of greatest importance for aquarists come primarily from Central and South America and from Africa.

Many aquarists create tanks with cichlid species from one particular area—for example, Lake Malawi, Lake Tanganyika, or Lake Victoria. There are so many different species in these lakes that it is not difficult to create a community aquarium.

139. Cichlids: What conditions must I provide if I want to keep cichlids in my aquarium?

Individual cichlid species have different husbandry requirements, depending on where they come from.
➤ The West African cichlids are often very colorful fish of small to medium size that come from the streams, rivers, and lakes of West and Central Africa. The water there is usually soft and acidic.
➤ The East African cichlids come primarily from Lake Tanganyika and Lake Malawi, which are also called rift lakes or alkali lakes. The water there is moderately hard to hard and alkaline.
➤ The cichlids from Central and South America inhabit very different types of water, which must be taken into account when caring for them.
➤ Cichlids from Central America are usually relatively large and quite aggressive, so they should be kept in a species aquarium.
➤ Many of the most popular cichlids come from South America. They include dwarf cichlids like the Ram (*Mikrogeophagus ramirezi*), as well as some of larger cichlids like discus (*Symphysodon* spp.), Angelfish (*Pterophyllum scalare*), and so-called earth-eaters (*Geophagus* spp.). These fish are found in the

INFO

Parental care in cichlids
There are the so-called parental families, in which both the father and the mother care for the young, seen for example in the Angelfish, and matriarchal families, in which only the mother fish takes care of the offspring, for example the Southern Mouthbreeder (*Pseudocrenilabrus philander*). It is rare among cichlids for the father to care for the offspring by himself, but this type of patriarchal family can be seen in the Blackchin Tilapia (*Sarotherodon melanotheron*).

enormous river systems of South America, most of which have soft, acidic water.

As far as feeding is concerned, you must keep in mind that almost all cichlids are predators. That is why you have to give them live or frozen foods regularly (at least once a week) in addition to dry foods.

140. Cichlids: Which parental care behaviors can I observe in cichlids?

Cichlids are fascinating, not just for their colors but also because of their breeding behavior. Generally speaking, all cichlids care for their offspring, although in a variety of ways. They can be divided into cave breeders, open breeders, and mouthbreeders, although the transitions between these groups can be fluid.

Cave breeders lay their eggs in hiding places like caves or recesses, while open breeders lay their eggs in the open on a substrate (plants, rocks). Mouthbreeders, in contrast, shelter their young in their mouths.

141. Clown Loaches: In my 20-gallon (80 L) community tank, I have a Clown Loach whose partner has died. Do I have to get my fish a new partner?

Clown Loaches (*Chromobotia macracanthus*) are schooling fish and should never be kept alone. You should keep at least five fish of this species. However, a 20-gallon (80-L) aquarium is too small for keeping Clown Loaches. They need an aquarium at least 80 inches (200 cm) long since they can grow up to 12 inches (30 cm) in length. Therefore, you should either get several Clown Loaches and a tank large enough to hold them or else give the solitary fish to another aquarist who is already keeping Clown Loaches in a tank of suitable proportions.

C

142. Cold-water Fish: I would like to set up a cold-water tank without a heater. Which ornamental fish are cold-water fish?

Ornamental fish that are happiest at lower temperatures include Goldfish (*Carassius auratus auratus*), sunfish (*Lepomis* spp.), Ide (*Leuciscus idus*), Three-spined Stickleback (*Gasterosteus aculeatus*), Belica (*Leucaspius delineatus*), and all other cold-water fish. You can certainly keep these species in an unheated aquarium indoors. Koi (*Cyprinus carpio*) are also cold-water fish, although they get too big for an indoor aquarium. They are happier in a garden pond. In the summer, make sure that the aquarium is protected from the sun so that the water temperature does not climb. The fish mentioned above can also be kept year-round in a garden pond if it is deep enough.

143. Communities: Which guidelines should I follow if I want to keep different species of fish together in a community?

Fish can be incompatible for a variety of reasons. When setting up a community aquarium, you should observe the following guidelines.
➤ Same size: In principle, it is not a good idea to keep fish of different sizes in the same tank. Even peaceful species can regard any fish that fits in its mouth as food. With decidedly predatory fish, just a slight

Black Ruby Barbs (Puntius nigrofasciatus) are among the more robust species for the community aquarium.

COMMUNITY AQUARIUM

An aquarium with a well-chosen community of fish is a real pleasure. Before you buy any fish, though, you need to find out if the species you would like to keep in your tank are

RED RAINBOWFISH

These lively rainbowfish are most active in the early morning, which is also when they display their most intense colors.

The Red Rainbowfish (*Glossolepis incisus*) grows up to 6 inches (15 cm) long and is a schooling fish. It gets along well with bottom-dwelling species.

BLACKLINE PENGUINFISH

The Blackline Penguinfish (*Thayeria boehlkei*), 2 ½ inches (6 cm) long, is a characin. Like most members of this family, it is definitely a schooling fish.

For this reason, you should keep at least six, preferably ten, of these fish. This active swimmer needs a large tank. Catfish and dwarf cichlids are compatible with characins.

HEAD-AND-TAILLIGHT TETRA

Head-and-taillight Tetras (*Hemigrammus ocellifer*), which get to be only about 2 inches (5 cm) long, are a beautiful sight with

their highly reflective colors. These lively schooling fish get along well with small bottom dwellers, surface swimmers, and dwarf cichlids. A large aquarium is important for keeping them in a community.

compatible. Things to keep in mind are the water parameters and amount of space they require as well as their size and behavior patterns, including territorial defense, parental care, schooling, and feeding.

RUMMYNOSE TETRA

The Rummynose Tetra (*Hemigrammus bleheri*) grows to be only about 1¾ inches (4.5 cm) long. It is also a schooling fish.

In the wild, Rummynose Tetras swim around in small groups or schools looking for microscopic prey in the open water. The delicate colors of this characin show off best against a dark background.

WAGTAIL PLATY

The red Wagtail Platy gets about 2½ inches (6 cm) long and comes from Mexico and Guatemala. Platies (*Xiphophorus maculatus*) belong to the live-bearing toothcarp family and are lively fish. They are compatible with bottom dwellers or other peaceful schooling fish.

ZEBRA PLECO

Suckermouth armored catfish, or plecos, are found in almost every community tank. They make an interesting contrast to

the colorful schooling fish. The Zebra Pleco (*Hypancistrus zebra*) grows up to 4½ inches (11 cm) long. Its behavior toward other fish is quiet and peaceful. A hiding place is especially important for this fish.

difference in body size is often all that is needed for the smaller fish to wind up as dinner. Predatory aquarium fish include cichlids, gobies, killifish, and some catfish, including air-breathing catfish.

➤ Similar water quality requirements: Fish have very different water quality requirements. For example, soft-water fish need soft water, and hard-water fish can thrive in only hard water. Do not put fish with different requirements into the same tank, or you will not be keeping any of the fish under the proper conditions.

➤ No fish that will injure each other: Some fish species like Tiger Barbs like to nip at the fins of other fish, especially the long-finned types. Consequently, they should not be kept in a community with long-finned or veiltail varieties.

➤ Similar feeding behavior: Fish that eat at a leisurely pace should not be kept with fish that feed greedily. Redchin Panchax (*Epiplatys dageti*), for example, are surface swimmers and quickly devour any food put into the aquarium. If bottom-dwelling fish are in the same tank, for example Masked Corys (*Corydoras metae*), then you have to be sure to put enough food into the aquarium so that some of it sinks to the bottom for the catfish.

➤ Different swimming levels: Do not stock an aquarium only with bottom dwellers or only with fish that all swim near the water surface. You will make much better use of the aquarium space if you put in species that occupy different water levels.

144. **Communities: I have Neon Tetras, Guppies, and a catfish in my 15-gallon (60 L) aquarium. I have to keep buying more Neons and Guppies, though, because they disappear without a trace. What is going on?**

You should act fast and find out what species of catfish you have, or ask your pet dealer for help. Your catfish might be a North American freshwater catfish (*Ictalu-*

rus spp.), a Frogmouth Catfish (*Chaca chaca*), a Lima Shovelnose Catfish (*Sorubim lima*), or an air-breathing catfish (*Clarias* spp.). These fish are predators and will view Neons and Guppies as welcome additions to the menu. If you have one of the above-mentioned species, you should find your catfish a new owner who keeps fish that are much bigger than the catfish. Alternatively, you can buy a second aquarium and keep the fish in separate tanks.

145. Communities: What animals besides fish can be kept in an aquarium?

In principle, you can keep many species of aquatic amphibians like Axolotls, African Clawed Frogs, or Rubber Eels as well as various crustaceans, aquatic insects, mussels, and snails in an aquarium. However, keeping them in a community with fish is only possible under certain conditions.

➤ Because of their unusual appearance, freshwater shrimp and crawfish are kept increasingly often with fish in the community aquarium. However, only

The Singapore Flower Shrimp is suitable for keeping in a community aquarium with small fish species.

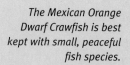

The Mexican Orange Dwarf Crawfish is best kept with small, peaceful fish species.

crustaceans that stay small are suitable for community tanks, for example Singapore Flower Shrimp and various species of dwarf shrimp. The fish also have to be peaceable and small.

➤ You can keep African dwarf frogs (*Hymenochirus* spp.) in a community tank together with small, peaceful fish like live-bearing toothcarps. The frogs need a water temperature of 71–75°F (22–24°C); water quality (°dGH, pH) is less important as long as the organic load is not too high (nitrate, nitrite, and ammonia). Feed African dwarf frogs with tiny frozen or live foods (water fleas, brine shrimp, or tubifex worms).

➤ Many snail species, like the Apple Snail (*Ampullaria gigas*), have proven to be good members of an aquarium community.

➤ Rubber Eels (*Typhlonectes* spp.) are amphibians and do not get along with aggressive, medium-size fish like Striped Panchax. These aquatic caecilians are also sold in pet stores as Sicilian Worms.

➤ If you want to keep pond turtles along with your fish in a community tank, the only possibility is the Common Musk Turtle (*Sternotherus odoratus*), which stays small. You have to feed them earthworms, snails, raw fish, and turtle pellets, though, so that they do not go after your fish. Sick or slow fish can still become prey for turtles. On the other hand, the turtles' waste products can foul the water severely, necessitating a powerful filter and regular water changes at least once a week.

146. **Communities: Which other aquarium animals are unsuitable or even dangerous to keep in a community tank with fish?**

➤ Larger crustaceans over $2^1/_2$ inches (6 cm) long usually prey on fish and therefore should never be kept with them in a community tank. Besides, larger species like *Procambarus clarkia*, a crawfish that can grow up to 6 inches (15 cm) long, will quickly devour all the aquarium plants. Crustaceans like this can be kept only in species tanks.

➤ Adult clawed frogs (*Xenopus* spp.) are also greedy predators and can even swallow relatively large fish with no trouble.

➤ Large Axolotls are dangerous for the fish, while the smaller ones are often attacked by them. Tiger Barbs (*Puntius tetrazona*) like to nip at the Axolotl's external gills, which can lead to infected wounds or even death.

➤ Pond turtles are often sold as tiny babies in pet stores, where they are sometimes kept in a tank with fish. However, do not let this tempt you to buy one on impulse. These cute little babies grow quickly with proper care, and depending on the species, can reach a shell length of up to 12 inches (30 cm). They need large tanks with a capacity of 125–250 gallons (500–1,000 L) or more. Only a few species are suitable for keeping in a community tank with fish.

➤ Larger pond turtles like Snapping Turtles and Alligator Snapping Turtles, which feed exclusively on fish, would devour your pets in no time.

147. Community Aquarium: What is meant by a community aquarium?

A community aquarium contains fish species that have similar requirements for conditions like water quality and temperature. It really does not matter if they come from different continents. The same holds true for plants. Which fish to group is a matter of taste, provided a few basic guidelines are observed when setting up the community. Of course, you can also create community aquariums with fish from one geographical area—for example, from Lake Malawi, Lake Tanganyika, or Lake Victoria, all of which contain large numbers of cichlid species.

148. Cyprinids: What are cyprinids, and which species of fish belong to this group?

The cyprinid family (Cyprinidae) includes several different groups of carplike fish. The cyprinids include more species than any other fish family. Cyprinids are found everywhere in the world except for South America and Australia.

They are characterized by a small number of teeth arranged in one to three rows on the lower pharyngeal bones (pharyngeal teeth) and a horny masticating plate located at the base of the pharyngeal bones, which is used to grind their food. Some species have barbels. Their swim bladder is divided into two chambers.

Many cyprinids are schooling fish and must be kept with several others of their species. They inhabit a wide variety of aquatic habitats, from fast-flowing streams to small ponds. Most cyprinids are omnivores. They are usually egg scatterers, which means they simply release their eggs into the open water and give their offspring no further care.

Familiar representative of the cyprinids are barbs like the Rosy Barb (*Puntius conchonius*), Tiger Barb (*Puntius tetrazona*), Black Ruby Barb (*Puntius nigrofasciatus*), Green Barb (*Puntius semifasciolatus*), and Cherry Barb (*Puntius titteya*). Other members of this family are danios and rasboras like the Zebra Danio (*Danio rerio*, formerly *Brachydanio rerio*) and Harlequin Rasbora (*Trigonostigma heteromorpha*, formerly *Rasbora heteromorpha*), White Cloud Mountain Minnows (*Tanichthys albonubes*), Red-tailed Black Sharks (*Epalzeorhynchos bicolor*, formerly *Labeo bicolor*), loaches like the Clown Loach (*Chromobotia macracanthus*) and Tiger Loach (*Botia hymenophysa*), Goldfish (*Carassius auratus auratus*), Ide (*Leuciscus idus*), Crucian Carp (*Carassius carassius*), and Koi (*Cyprinus carpio*).

149. Fighting Fish: **Are fighting fish really so aggressive, and can I keep them with other species in the aquarium?**

Fighting fish, or bettas, are not at all aggressive toward other fish species. Quite the contrary, when kept together with very lively fish, they are often rather shy and retreat to hiding places. However, the males of many betta species fight with each other, sometimes to the death of one of them. There are different species of bettas with different degrees of aggressiveness. The veiltail Siamese Fighting Fish are not very aggressive, while the short-finned fish that are bred in Thailand for illegal competitions are extremely pugnacious. The varieties sold in pet stores are almost exclusively veiltails, because they are more attractive.

150. Fish: **How long have fish existed on Earth and what characterizes them, biologically speaking?**

Fish (Pisces) are cold-blooded (poikilothermic) aquatic vertebrates. They are the oldest vertebrates on Earth. Many different types of fish were already living on Earth 450 million years ago, during the Silurian Period. With over 24,000 species, fish have more species than any other group of vertebrates.

Fish are characterized by their typical spindle-shaped body, which is divided into a head, trunk, tail, and fins. Of course, many species deviate considerably from this spindle shape in order to adapt to a particular habitat. For example, the flattened body shape of skates and rays is perfectly suited to a bottom-dwelling lifestyle. There is also tremendous variation in the size of fish. Some fish measure just $1/3$ inch (1 cm) long when fully grown, like the Dwarf Goby from the Philippines (*Trimmatom nanus*). In contrast, others like the Whale Shark (*Rhinodon typicus*, now known as *Rhincodon typus*) can reach a length of over 50 feet (15 m). Fish use gills to extract all or at least most of the oxygen they require from the water. They inhabit almost every body of water in the world, whether they be cold mountain streams, brackish-water zones, the ocean, large lakes, ponds, or the tiniest pools and ditches. Fish can be found in the abyssal ocean at depths of over 3,300 feet (1,000 m) as well as in mountain lakes at altitudes above 16,500 feet (5,000 m).

151. Goldfish and Koi: Young Koi and Goldfish often look very much alike. How can I tell them apart?

At first glance, distinguishing between young Koi and Goldfish sometimes seems difficult. However, Koi have two clearly visible barbels on the mouth that are absent in Goldfish. In addition, certain colors and patterns are found only in Koi. Adult fish are unmistakably different in size. Koi can grow to be over 3 feet (1 m) long, while Goldfish reach a maximum length of 12 inches (30 cm).

152. Keeping Fighting Fish: I am fascinated by the behavior of fighting fish. What must I take into consideration when keeping them?

Fighting fish are beautiful to watch in a species aquarium. The tank does not have to be very large, but should have a volume of at least 15 gallons (60 L).
➤ Keep one male with two or three females.
➤ To keep the water clean, install a small filter that does not produce a very strong current. Fighting fish need warm water, so the aquarium must be heated. The water temperature should be 79–82°F (26–28°C).

➤ Many fighting fish do not readily accept dry foods, so you should offer them live or frozen foods once or twice a week.

➤ The tank should have a few floating plants so the male can anchor his bubble nest. A handful of Java Moss and a few hiding places are necessary so that the female can dodge the male, who tends to get a bit rough during courtship. You can observe the courtship

Bettas like these Siamese Fighting Fish (Betta splendens) *look their best in a species aquarium.*

and display behavior of bettas very nicely in a species aquarium. With a bit of luck, you can also see the interesting parental care these fish exercise, which includes building a bubble nest and rearing the young. After spawning, the male guards the eggs and later the fry. If they fall out of the bubble nest, he picks them up in his mouth and spits them back into the nest. Since the male now regards the female as an unwelcome intruder and attacks her, you should transfer the female to another aquarium after she lays her eggs. Otherwise, she could be chased and killed by an aggressive male guarding his offspring.

153. Killifish: What exactly are killifish?

The name killifish refers to the egg-laying tooth-carps, also known as cyprinodonts. Killifish include many different genera and more than 480 species. They are found in temperate to tropical regions throughout the world with the exception of Australia.

The name killifish is derived from the Old Dutch word "kil," which means *small watercourse*. Many killifish live in permanent streams and brackish-water zones. As adhesive spawners and plant spawners, they prefer to lay their eggs on fine-leaved plants or tangled roots.

On the other hand, some killifish live in regions with alternating dry and rainy seasons. The habitat of these killifish—usually small bodies of water—dries up seasonally. This results in the death of the adult fish, but their eggs survive the dry period buried in the muddy bottom. The young fish hatch the next time it rains, although a few offspring of the same clutch wait until the second or third rainy period. Killifish like this that lay their eggs in the substrate (substrate spawners) and then die with the onset of the dry season are also called annual fish. The different species vary greatly in appearance. They range in size from 1 inch (2.5 cm) to over 12 inches (30 cm) long, with most species reaching a length of about 2–2½ inches (5–6 cm). The males are usually more colorful than the females.

154. Killifish: What must I take into consideration if I keep killifish in my aquarium?

Since killifish inhabit a variety of biotopes, the individual species have very different husbandry requirements. Most killifish prefer soft, slightly acidic water. A few species must be kept in hard alkaline water, like *Lamprichthys tanganicanus* from Lake Tanganyika. As a rule, killifish prefer live foods. Many species accept dry foods reluctantly if at all.

Even under optimal aquarium conditions, many killifish do not live very long—only 1.5 years on average. Depending on the species, life expectancy varies from 12 months to 5 years. So-called annual fish like *Cynolebias* spp., *Nothobranchius* spp., and *Pterolebias* spp. often do not live much more than a year.

Depending on the species and natural habitat, killifish require temperatures between 68 and 86°F (20 and 30°C), a densely planted tank with places to hide, clumps of fine-leaved plants, bundles of peat fibers as a spawning substrate, and a tight-fitting cover glass because most killifish are extremely good jumpers.

Many killifish like the Redtail Notho (*Nothobranchius guentheri*) or Longfin Killie (*Pterolebias longipinnis*) have to be kept in species aquariums because they have very special requirements. Killifish like the Striped Panchax (*Aplocheilus lineatus*) can definitely be kept in a community tank but only if all the other fish in the tank are distinctly larger. Almost all killifish are predators and will regard any smaller fish as dinner.

The most popular killifish for the aquarium include the Striped Panchax (*Aplocheilus lineatus*), Redchin Panchax (*Epiplatys dageti*), Lampeye Panchax (*Aplocheilichthys macrophthalmus*), Cuban Rivulus (*Rivulus cylindraceus*), and colorful species like the Blue Gularis (*Aphyosemion sjoestedti*).

155. Labyrinth Fish: What are labyrinth fish, and why are they called that?

Labyrinth fish, also known as anabantids, get their name from their accessory breathing apparatus, the so-called labyrinth organ. They can use this organ to take in atmospheric air from the water surface. Labyrinth fish must always have access to the water surface, or they will asphyxiate. Because of this accessory breathing method, they can live in even oxygen-poor environments where excessive warming of shallow water or heavy organic pollution have reduced oxygen levels.

Labyrinth fish are native to Africa and Asia. They include bettas like the Siamese Fighting Fish (*Betta splendens*), gouramis like the Pearl Gourami (*Tri-*

chogaster leeri) and Kissing Gourami (*Helostoma temminckii*), and Paradise Fish (*Macropodus opercularis*). Most labyrinth fish take care of their offspring. Many typically construct a bubble nest at the water surface where the eggs and newly hatched fry are tended by the male. There are also cave breeders like the Spike-tailed Paradise Fish (*Pseudosphromenus dayi*), which build their bubble nests in small caves, and mouth breeders like the Chocolate Gourami (*Sphaerichthys osphromenoides*).

156. Labyrinth Fish: What are the requirements for keeping labyrinth fish in an aquarium?

Labyrinth fish can usually be kept well in neutral to slightly acidic water that is not too hard. The tank should be heavily planted in places so that the female can retreat if the male pesters her too much. I also recommend a few floating plants for bubble nest builders. They will eagerly use these to anchor their bubble nests. You should provide flowerpots or coconut shells for cave breeders. The flow produced by the filter should be very gentle since labyrinth fish come predominantly from stagnant waters and do not like too much current. Besides, strong currents destroy the bubble nests.

With some species, for instance the Kissing Gourami, you can keep two or more males in the same tank. Most species, especially the Siamese Fighting Fish (*Betta splendens*), should be kept only as a pair or as one male with two or three females; otherwise the males will fight to the death.

Labyrinth fish usually accept dry foods, but they should still get live or frozen foods at least once a week.

Most labyrinth fish can be kept in a tank with quiet fish that also require soft to medium-hard water and are neither too aggressive nor very small.

157. Lake Malawi Tank: I would like to set up a Lake Malawi tank. What do I have to keep in mind when doing this?

You should keep only fish from Lake Malawi in a tank like this. Lake Malawi is an East African rift lake about 400 miles (700 km) long. In order to create a miniature version of the Lake Malawi community using three to five species of fish, you will need an aquarium over 48 inches (120 cm) long. Then you can set up rock structures and sandy areas as well as open-water zones. The most important habitat is the rock zone. The water should be hard (15–20 °dH) and alkaline (pH 7.1–8.5). The temperature should stay between 75 and 79°F (24 and 26°C).

Suitable cichlids from Lake Malawi include the peacock cichlids (*Aulonocara* spp.), hump-heads (*Cyrtocara* spp.), and the smaller tilapias (*Tilapia* spp.). If you keep several species of cichlids together, you should make sure that the fish are all about the same

The only inhabitants in a Lake Malawi tank are cichlids native to these waters.

size and have similar temperaments. Much smaller species are often terrorized by the larger ones. In addition, aquarists usually prefer to keep cichlids as pairs. Rocks are the best thing to use for aquascaping. If you want to build a rocky wall in the aquarium, be sure to glue the rocks together with aquarium silicone sealant. If the structure collapses, the fish can be injured and the aquarium glass can even break. Never use bogwood for aquascaping. It releases humic acids that acidify the water, something the fish from Lake Malawi cannot tolerate.

158. Live-bearing Toothcarps: What does *live-bearing toothcarp* mean, and which fish belong to this group?

The unusual characteristic of live-bearing toothcarps is the way they reproduce. Live-bearing toothcarps give birth to live young following internal fertilization. The males use their modified anal fin, called a gonopodium, to transfer sperm packets to the females. The gestation period in most live-bearing toothcarps is 4–6 weeks. The number of fry varies from 2–100 per brood, depending on the species, age, and size of the female. The female can store the sperm in her body after mating and use it to give birth to several broods in succession. Thus you may suddenly find baby fish swimming around in your aquarium although no male is present. The natural distribution range of live-bearing toothcarps extends from southern North America across Central America (including the Caribbean Islands) to South America. Guppies (*Poecilia reticulata*, formerly known as *Lebistes reticulata*) and Mosquito Fish (*Gambusia affinis*), in particular, were used even outside the Americas to destroy mosquito larvae in an attempt to control malaria. Now they can be found in tropical areas throughout the world. Live-bearing toothcarps include many popular aquarium fish like Guppies (*Poecilia reticulata*), Swordtails (*Xiphophorus hellerii*), Mollies (*Poecilia sphenops*), Platies (*Xiphophorus maculatus*), and Sailfin Mollies (*Poecilia velifera*). There are several reasons for the popularity of this group. They are often very colorful and come in attractive varieties. In addition, they are relatively robust, easy to breed, and get along well with other fish in a community aquarium.

159. Live-bearing Toothcarps: What should I bear in mind if I want to keep live-bearing toothcarps? **?**

Most live-bearing toothcarps should be kept in neutral and moderately hard to hard water. However, many wild-caught and captive-bred fish from Southeast Asia prefer soft water. Mollies are also found in brackish water, so it is often good for these fish if you add salt to the water. Heavily planted areas and a few floating plants offer hiding places for the fry and should be present in any tank with live-bearers.

1 *Variable Platies (*Xiphophorus variatus*) are live-bearers and grow up to 2½ inches (6 cm) long. There are many varieties.*

2 *Swordtails (*Xiphophorus hellerii*) owe their name to the elongated lower edge of their caudal fin.*

All species of live-bearing toothcarps are gregarious, so you should always have several fish of the same species. There should be two to four females for every male to prevent the females from being harassed and overly stressed by the males, who are always ready to mate.

When feeding, keep in mind that most live-bearing toothcarps prefer vegetable food. For this reason, you should feed dry foods containing vegetable matter. You can also allow the green algae to grow on the back wall and the decorations; it is a welcome supplement to their diet. Once or twice a week, you can also give them live or frozen foods like mosquito larvae or water fleas.

160. Mudskippers: I would like to keep Mudskippers. How difficult is it to keep these fish?

Mudskippers (*Periophthalmus barbarus*) are very interesting fish indeed but quite difficult to keep and suitable for only advanced aquarists.

They inhabit the intertidal zone of tropical lakes, particularly mangrove swamps. These fish live at the boundary between land and water. When the water level drops, they burrow into the muddy bottom. For this reason, they need a spacious tank with a soft, sandy substrate in at least one area and a sort of beach as well as branches to climb on.

An aquarium with Mudskippers also needs a powerful filter that can handle all the dirt these fish stir up by burrowing. You have to cover the aquarium well so that the humidity stays high and the fish's skin does not dry out. Mudskippers primarily eat live foods like worms and, in particular, insects.

161. Native Fish: I have a cool room in the basement where I would like to set up a 25-gallon (100 L) tank so I can keep and observe cold-water fish. Which species would you recommend?

For a 25-gallon (100 L) aquarium, I would suggest you select fish species that stay small. Three-spined Sticklebacks (*Gasterosteus aculeatus*) and Bitterlings (*Rhodeus sericeus amarus*) are both wonderful to observe because of their interesting breeding behavior.

➤ The male Stickleback assumes his brilliant breeding colors in spring during the mating season. He builds a nest where the female lays her eggs. The male fertilizes them and then guards the clutch.

➤ In Bitterlings, the male looks for a Painter's Mussel or other fresh-water mussel in which the female can lay her eggs. She does this using her breeding tube, which she develops during the mating season. The eggs and the newly hatched fry are protected from predators inside the mussel.

Deposition of the Bitterling's eggs also has an advantage for the mussel: The mussel larvae (glochidia) attach themselves to the newly hatched Bitterling fry like parasites and then develop into little mussels on the skin of their hosts. The fish also serve as a safe method of transportation for the baby mussels and thus ensure their dispersal. After two to ten weeks, the mussels leave their host Bitterlings.

➤ Other small cyprinids worth considering for a 25-gallon (100 L) aquarium are the Eurasian Minnow (*Phoxinus phoxinus*) and the Belica (*Leucaspius delineatus*). However, if you keep Eurasian Minnows, you must be sure to provide them with relatively oxygen-rich water, because this species comes from fast-moving streams.

162. Oscars: What exactly is this fish known as the Oscar?

Oscar is the name used by aquarists for the Peacock Cichlid (*Astronotus ocellatus*), a member of the cichlid family (Cichlidae). Oscars come from the Amazon Basin in South America and grow to be over 12 inches (30 cm) in length. For this reason, they are suitable for only very large aquariums more than 80 inches (2 m) long. When kept under the right conditions in an appropriately large tank, these fish can be kept together with other peaceful giants, like large sucker-mouth armored catfish. Feed them cichlid sticks, feeder fish, earthworms, and crustaceans.

163. Paludarium: What is a paludarium, and which animals can be kept in a system like this?

A paludarium is also called a swamp aquarium. It consists of a planted land area with a shoreline and a water zone. You could also say that it is a combination of aquarium (lower part of the paludarium) and terrarium (upper part). This hybrid form makes it possible to keep fish, amphibians, and certain reptiles at the same time.

164. Piranhas: Are piranhas really as dangerous as they are rumored to be?

Piranhas have lots of sharp teeth and can even injure human skin. However, the dangerous nature of these fish is greatly exaggerated. Piranhas become aggressive when they smell blood or detect unusual movements suggesting an injured fish that would be easy prey. However, it is certainly not realistic to think that they can skeletonize a human hand in seconds.

Feeder fish or weakened companions, however, are quickly stripped to the bone. When you are working in the aquarium, wear rubber gloves and move your hands slowly.

165. Pufferfish: Is buying a pufferfish for a community tank a good idea for biological control of snails?

Pufferfish (*Tetraodon* spp.) are suitable for keeping only in a species aquarium, since they can attack, injure, or even kill other fish. I recommend you do not buy a puffer, because you will certainly have problems with it in your community tank. Besides, many of the pufferfish species offered for sale are brackish-water fish and cannot be properly kept in a normal freshwater aquarium for any length of time.

166. Rainbowfish: Where do rainbowfish come from, and which fish belong to this family?

Rainbowfish (family Melanotaeniidae) are native to northern Australia, Papua New Guinea, and a few offshore islands. There are about 50 different species. Normally, they are rather small, measuring up to $6^{3}/_{4}$ inches (17 cm) long.

INFO

Rainbowfish
They are among the most beautiful of all aquarium fish. Pet stores frequently carry Boeseman's Rainbowfish (*Melanotaenia boesemani*), Red Rainbowfish (*Glossolepis incisus*), Macculloch's Rainbowfish (*Melanotaenia maccullochi*), Banded Rainbowfish (*Melanotaenia trifasciata*), and Dwarf Rainbowfish (*Melanotaenia praecox*).

They live in rivers, lakes, and swamps, with a few representatives inhabiting brackish water as well. Their shape is elongated, and older males are often deep bodied. They are adaptable and for the most part peaceful.

Since they are usually schooling fish, you should always keep at least five rainbowfish of the same species in an aquarium. You need to provide plenty of open swimming space in an aquarium for rainbow fish. The foreground should be left unplanted or have only very low-growing plants. Keep these fish in hard, neutral to slightly alkaline water. Feed them dry foods supplemented once or twice a week with live or frozen foods.

Rainbowfish can be kept together with other peaceful, quiet fish that also prefer medium–hard to hard water.

167. Rays: I really like rays. Can I keep them in the aquarium? ?

Most rays live in salt water and get to be very large. Consequently, they are suitable only for display tanks in places like zoos.

Although freshwater rays stay somewhat smaller, they still reach a length of over 32 inches (80 cm). Full-grown animals require a tank with a minimum capacity of 500 gallons (2,000 L) and as large a bottom area as possible.

Only if you have the space and the financial means for a tank like this does it make sense to get rays. Besides, handling rays can be dangerous. They have a venomous spine that can cause serious injury even to humans. Since freshwater rays are demanding pets, you should have acquired plenty of experience with other fish before you get one.

168. Schooling Fish: Why are schooling fish kept in large group?

Schooling fish need the company of others of their kind because only then can they display the behavior typical of their species. You should keep schooling fish in groups of at least six to ten animals. They are unhappy by themselves and will pine away or even become aggressive toward other species.

Fish usually form schools in order to protect themselves from predators. It is difficult for a predator to single out and capture one fish in a school.

Schooling fish include:

➤ Characins like the Neon Tetra (*Paracheirodon innesi*) or Flame Tetra (*Hyphessobrycon flammeus*),

➤ Rainbowfish like the Dwarf Rainbowfish (*Melanotaenia praecox*) and Boeseman's Rainbowfish (*Melanotaenia boesemani*),

➤ Danios and rasboras like the Zebra Danio (*Danio rerio*) and the Harlequin Rasbora (*Trigonostigma heteromorpha*),

➤ Many species of barbs like the Black Ruby Barb (*Puntius nigrofasciatus*) and Tiger Barb (*Puntius tetrazona*).

169. Shark Catfish: I really like the so-called shark catfish. What sort of fish are these, and is buying some a good idea?

These are not sharks (which are cartilaginous fish) but, rather, bony fish that belong to the sea catfish family.

This group includes the Tete Sea Catfish (*Ariopsis seemanni*), also known to aquarists as the Colombian Shark. Although these fish are very attractive, I advise you against buying any shark catfish, because they can grow, to be more than 20 inches (50 cm) long.

Besides, when fully grown, they become predatory loners. As brackish-water fish, they also need a marine salt supplement in the aquarium water.

170. Single-specimen Tanks: I have seen an aquarium containing just one fish. Should some fish be kept by themselves in a tank?

With some species of ornamental fish, you can keep only one specimen in an aquarium because both the males as well as the females are highly territorial. One fish that displays this kind of behavior is the Red-tailed Black Shark (*Epalzeorhynchos bicolor*), which absolutely cannot be kept with others of its kind.

171. Size of Fish: Which fish become too large for the average aquarium?

Although only a few centimeters long as babies, some fish can become absolute giants when fully grown. These include the Clown Loach (*Chromobotia macracanthus*), the Oscar (*Astronotus ocellatus*) and other large cichlids like the Chanchito (*Australoheros facetus*) and the Texas Cichlid (*Herichthys cyanoguttatus*), the Colombian Shark (*Ariopsis seemanni*), air-breathing catfish (*Clarias* spp.), lungfish like African lungfish of the genus *Protopterus*, and many catfish like Commerson's Suckermouth Catfish (*Hypostomus commersoni*) and the Lima Shovelnose Catfish (*Sorubim lima*).

To avoid any unpleasant surprises, you should find out how big a fish grows before you buy it. Ask for the scientific name so you can identify the species correctly. If a particular species will grow too large to be comfortably housed in your aquarium, you should obviously avoid purchasing it.

172. Snails: Many aquariums contain snails in addition to fish. What role do they play?

Introducing unwanted snails or their eggs into your tank is not uncommon when you buy new plants. However, many aquarists deliberately put snails into the tank with their fish.

Although many species of snails do eat algae and polish off uneaten food, they eliminate it again in the form of snail feces. In the end, they really do not help to keep the aquarium clean, because the excess organic matter remains in the aquarium. Many snail species can also cause problems because they go after the plants.

One popular and useful snail is the Malaysian Trumpet Snail (*Melanoides tuberculata*). These snails live primarily in the substrate, which they loosen up by their movements.

The large Apple Snail (*Ampullaria gigas*) has a shell that can grow up to 2½ inches (6 cm) in diameter and comes in a variety of colors. It is often kept in aquariums along with fish and is very decorative as well as interesting to watch.

Keeping snails in your tank is your decision since doing so has disadvantages as well as some advantages. If they colonize the aquarium in large numbers, they present an aesthetic problem for many aquarists.

The Red-tailed Black Shark (Epalzeorhynchos bicolor) *is a quarrelsome creature and cannot be kept with others of its kind.*

173. Species Aquarium: What is meant by a species aquarium, and is it suitable for beginners?

In contrast to a community aquarium, in which a variety of fish with similar husbandry requirements are kept, a species aquarium contains fish of only one species. The advantage of a species aquarium is that conditions can be precisely adjusted to suit the requirements of the occupants. Furthermore, many species can even be bred there, so setting up a special breeding tank is not necessary.

Many novice aquarists start out with a community tank since what they want most is a colorful aquarium with many different kinds of fish. The longer they continue to enjoy the fish-keeping hobby, the more likely they are to develop an interest in a particular family or species of fish. That is why, sooner or later, many advanced aquarists switch to species aquariums.

In principle, though, even beginners can keep a species aquarium, although they should not start by choosing a very demanding species like the Ram (*Mikrogeophagus ramirezi*).

Quite a few fish species are best kept in a species aquarium because they are susceptible to diseases in a community tank. Among these is the Discus. Most killifish, for example nothos (*Nothobranchius* spp.), are best kept in a species aquarium because of their special requirements. Very small species like dwarf live-bearers (*Neoheterandria* spp.) often languish in a community tank or are even eaten by other fish.

If you decide to set up a species aquarium do some homework first. Find out which species are most suitable for your level of expertise and your level of commitment. You do not want to end up with a tank full of fish that you cannot take care of for one reason or another.

174. Species Diversity: How many species of fish are actually in the world?

At present, there are about 25,000 different species of fish, with many new species still being discovered every year. The known species belong to over 400 families and are divided into two classes, each with two subclasses. These classes are cartilaginous fish and bony fish. Practically all the popular ornamental fish are bony fish. Cartilaginous fish number just under 400 species and include sharks, skates, rays, ratfish, and chimaeras. The zoological classification into cartilaginous and bony fish is based on differences in skeletal structure. Bony fish have a bony skeleton, while cartilaginous fish have one made of cartilage.

175. Species Diversity: How many of the known species are actually kept as ornamental fish in aquariums?

Of the 25,000 different species of fish, only about 2,000 species are more or less regularly sold as ornamental fish. The most important groups for the aquarium trade are characins, cyprinids, catfish, egg-laying toothcarps, live-bearing toothcarps, labyrinth fish, rainbowfish, and cichlids. All other fish species are either not attractive enough or else they get too large for a typical aquarium.

The Spotted Blue-Eye (Pseudomugil gertrudae), only 1½ inches (4 cm) long, is one of the species that stays small.

176. Species for Beginners: Which species of fish are suitable for me as a beginner? ?

If you have no experience in fish keeping, begin with the standard ornamental fish species that have been bred in captivity and are known to be relatively robust. These include Swordtails (*Xiphophorus hellerii*), Zebra Danios (*Danio rerio*), White Cloud Mountain Minnows (*Tanichthys albonubes*), Bronze Corydoras (*Corydoras aeneus*), Angelfish (*Pterophyllum scalare*), Rosy Barbs (*Puntius conchonius*), Paradise Fish (*Macropodus opercularis*), and Guppies (*Poecilia reticulata*). However, a beginner should not select fancy Guppies with elaborate finnage, because these are somewhat complicated to keep and not as robust as the "normal" Guppies.

177. Species for Small Aquariums: I have never owned an aquarium and would like to get a small 15-gallon (60 L) tank. Which fish can I keep in it as a beginner? ?

Only fish that stay small are suitable for a small aquarium. You can combine two or three species of fish if you make sure that they all have the same or at least similar requirements for water hardness and pH. You should not keep more than three species in a 15-gallon (60 L) tank. Suitable species include Cardinal Tetras (*Paracheirodon axelrodi*), Neon Tetras (*Paracheirodon innesi*), White Cloud Mountain Minnows (*Tanichthys albonubes*), Harlequin Rasboras (*Trigonostigma heteromorpha,* formerly known as *Rasbora heteromorpha*), Cory Catfish (*Corydoras* spp.), Starlight Bristlenose Catfish (*Ancistrus dolichopterus*), Guppies (*Poecilia reticulata*), Platies (*Xiphophorus maculatus*), Swordtails (*Xiphophorus hellerii*), and Zebra Danios (*Danio rerio*).

Small aquariums in particular should never be stocked with too many fish, because overcrowding can make the water quality deteriorate very quickly. You should also make sure that the fish occupy different swimming levels of the tank. With three species, you should have one bottom dweller, one midwater swimmer, and one surface-swimming species.

Here is one example of how you can set up your tank: five or six Guppies, Platies, or Swordtails (one or two males and three or four females), four Cory Catfish, a pair of bristlenose catfish, and two or three apple snails (e.g., *Ampullaria* spp.) in addition to the fish. The water should be medium hard to hard.

Suitable aquatic plants for this setup include Java Fern (*Microsorium pteropus*), Dwarf Hygrophila (*Hygrophila polysperma*), pondweed or elodea (*Egeria* spp.), Java Moss (*Vesicularia dubyana*), and Hornwort (*Ceratophyllum demersum*).

178. Species for Small Aquariums: I would like to set up a small tank (about 15 gallons/60 L) and stock it exclusively with very small fish. Which aquarium fish stay quite small?

If you would like fish that are small but elegant, here are some suggestions.

➤ You can combine Tiger Teddys (*Neoheterandria elegans*) with Dwarf Corydoras (*Corydoras hastatus*). Tiger Teddys are the smallest of the live-bearing toothcarps. The males scarcely get larger than $\frac{3}{4}$ inch (2 cm). The tank should be heavily planted, and the water should be medium-hard and have a neutral pH. You can keep two male and four female Tiger Teddys and five or six Dwarf Corydoras in the same tank.

➤ Bumblebee Gobies (*Hypogymnogobius xanthozona*) are very pretty and get to be only $1\frac{1}{2}$ inches (3.5 cm) long, but they need hard water and supplemental salt

(2–4 tablespoons per 5 gallons [30–60 mL per 20 L] of water). In addition, the aquarium must have plenty of cavelike hiding places. These fish require frequent feedings of small live and frozen foods since they usually do not accept dry foods.

You could keep four or five Bumblebee Gobies in a 15-gallon (60 L) aquarium, but you should not keep them together with other fish.

➤ Rosy Tetras (*Hyphessobrycon rosaceus*) are about 1¼ inches (3 cm) long. Keep about 12 fish of this species in the tank. These open-water swimmers are happiest at water temperatures of 75–79°F (24–26°C).

➤ Banded Panchax (*Pseudepiplatys annulatus*) grow to almost 1½ inches (4 cm) in length, swim in the upper water level, and prefer soft water. They must have floating plants in the tank to give them some protection from above. Banded Panchax can be kept together with Dwarf Corydoras. In a 15-gallon (60 L) tank, you can keep two male and three or four female Banded Panchax along with five Dwarf Corydoras.

The Banded Panchax is ideal for small tanks.

179. Stocking: Which basic factors must I keep in mind when I select fish for an aquarium?

A number of factors determine which fish are suitable for an aquarium.

➤ Tank size: Each fish needs a certain volume of water and an adequate amount of swimming space, depending on its body length. As a rule, only small fish can be kept in small tanks.

➤ Water quality: This is crucial for the well-being of your fish. If your tap water does not satisfy the needs of your fish and cannot be suitably conditioned, then please note the following. If your tap water is soft, you must choose fish that prefer soft water. These include many species of characins and South American cichlids. If your tap water is hard, then fish native to hard water will be suitable. These include rainbowfish, East African cichlids from Lake Malawi or Lake Tanganyika, and most live-bearing toothcarps, such as Mollies.

➤ Compatibility: Naturally, the fish must be able to get along and not attack each other. The husbandry requirements of the individual species must also be similar. Furthermore, you should stock the aquarium with fish that occupy different swimming levels, meaning the bottom, middle, and upper levels of the water.

180. Stocking Levels: How can I determine how many fish will fit in my aquarium?

If you would like to figure out how many fish will fit in an aquarium, you can usually do so with two basic rules. These keep in mind that both the volume of water available as well as the dimensions of the tank must suit the fish.

Every fish needs a certain volume of water depending on its size. As far as dimensions are concerned, the tank should be at least ten times as long and five times as wide as the body length of the longest fish. This is why finding out the adult size of a species when buying juvenile fish and always using this ultimate size as the basis for your calculations are important.

Of course, you do not have to adhere strictly to these rules of thumb because water quality also plays an important role in deciding how many fish you can keep. You can keep more fish in a well-maintained tank with plenty of plants where the fish are fed sparingly and filter performance is optimal than you can in a tank with inadequate filtration where important maintenance tasks like filter cleaning and water changes are carried out infrequently or where the fish are overfed.

The following guidelines for determining stocking levels are taken from the *Certificate of Proficiency in Freshwater Fishkeeping,* published by the Association of German Aquarium and Terrarium Clubs and the German Society for Herpetology and Terrarium Science.

➤ Fish up to 1 inch (2 cm) long need ⅔ gallon of water per inch (1 L per cm) of body length.

➤ Fish with a body length between 1 and 2 inches (2 and 5 cm) need 1 gallon of water per inch (1.5 L per cm) of body length.

➤ Fish with a body length between 2 and 4 inches (5 and 10 cm) need 1⅓ gallons of water per inch (2 L per cm) of body length.

➤ Fish with a body length between 4 and 6 inches (10 and 15 cm) need 2 gallons of water per inch (3 L per cm) of body length.

➤ Fish with a body length over 6 inches (15 cm) need 2⅔ gallons of water per inch (4 L per cm) of body length.

Along with these recommendations, please keep in mind the suggestions given on the required tank dimensions.

181. **Stocking Levels: I have a 38-gallon (145 L) aquarium. How can I stock this tank?**

The space and water requirements of the fish play a role in determining how you can stock an aquarium. Naturally, the species you select must also be compatible and have similar requirements. Since the tank decorations displace some of the water and the water level is a bit below the top of the aquarium anyway, you will have to subtract about 10–20 percent from the 38-gallon (145 L) capacity.

Assume, then, that you have about 31 gallons (120 L) of water available for your fish. The following two examples show how you can determine the possible stocking levels.

Example No. 1: All the fish are between 1 and 2 inches (2 and 5 cm) long, so you must multiply by 1 gallon/inch (1.5 L/cm).

➤ 4 Platies (*Xiphophorus maculatus*) require 6 gallons (24 L) of water, which you can calculate as follows.

EXTRA TIP

Less is more
Even if it is often difficult to limit yourself to a few species when stocking an aquarium—after all, there are so many beautiful fish that you would like to have—you should exercise some restraint. Do not overstock your tank. Overcrowding an aquarium causes more stress for the fish, a greater risk of infection, and consequently more health problems. You will derive lasting enjoyment from your fish only if the stocking levels are right.

The body length per Platy is 1.5 inches (4 cm). This is 1.5 × 1 gallon (4 × 1.5 L) per fish, or 1.5 gallons (6 L) of water per fish, which comes to a total of 6 gallons (24 L) for 4 Platies.

➤ 3 female and 2 male Guppies (*Poecilia reticulata*) require 7 gallons (27 L) of water. 3 females with a body length of 1.5 inches (4 cm), or 1.5 × 1 gallon (4 × 1.5 L) per female, equals 1.5 gallons (6 L) of water. This is 4.5 gallons (18 L) for 3 females. 2 males with a body length of 1.25 inches (3 cm), or 1.25 × 1 gallon (3 × 1.5 L) per male, equals 1.25 gallons (4.5 L) of water. Which is 2.5 gallons (9 L) for 2 males.

➤ 4 Mollies (*Poecilia sphenops*) require 6 gallons (24 L) of water. Body length of the Molly is 1.5 inches (4 cm), so the water required per Molly is 1.5 × 1 gallon (4 × 1.5 L) = 1.5 gallons (6 L). This is 6 gallons (24 L) for 4 Mollies.

➤ 6 Cory Catfish (*Corydoras* spp.) require 12 gallons (45 L) of water. Body length of the Cory is 2 inches (5 cm), so the water required per catfish is 2 × 1 gallon (5 × 1.5 L) = 2 gallons (7.5 L). This is 12 gallons (45 L) for 6 catfish.

If you now add up the volumes of water required by the individual groups of fish, you get 31 gallons (120 L).

Example No. 2: The fish are 5 inches (13 cm) and 5.5 inches (14 cm) long, so you have to multiply by 2 gallons/inch (3 L/cm):

➤ 2 Keyhole Cichlids (*Aequidens maronii*) with a body length of 5 inches (13 cm). This yields a water requirement of 5 × 2 = 10 gallons (13 × 3 = 39 L) per fish, which is 20 gallons (78 L) for the two cichlids.

➤ 1 Banjo Catfish (*Bunocephalus coracoideus*) with a body length of 5.5 inches (14 cm), which requires 5.5 × 2 = 11 gallons (14 × 3 = 42 L) of water.

182. Temperature: What water temperature do ornamental fish need in the aquarium?

Aquariums in which tropical ornamental fish are kept must be heated. Normal room temperature is too low for most ornamental fish. The water temperature of your aquarium is determined by which fish species you keep.

White Cloud Mountain Minnows like temperatures around 68°F (20°C). Most tropical fish prefer temperatures of 72–79°F (22–26°C). Discus and bettas, on the other hand, are happier at higher temperatures between 79 and 82°F (26 and 28°C).

Cold-water fish differ considerably in the temperatures they can tolerate. Sunfish, Eurasian Minnows, Belica, and sticklebacks can tolerate temperatures above 68°F (20°C) only briefly. Koi and Goldfish, which are frequently captive bred in warm regions and imported from there, can tolerate temperatures of 68°F (20°C) and above, even for lengthy periods. You do not need to heat aquariums for cold-water fish.

Feeding, Maintenance, and Water Quality

Your fish need a healthy
environment in order to feel their
best. In the following chapter,
you will find answers to questions
on aquarium maintenance, water
quality, and feeding.

183. Algae: Lately I have had algae growing in my aquarium. Is that a problem?

Moderate algae growth is normal and can even be good for your aquarium. Algae remove substances from the water that are harmful for fish. In addition, they give off oxygen when exposed to light. They are also a welcome change in the diet of many fish, for example live-bearing toothcarps and catfish. However, if algae get out of hand, this is not only unsightly but can also have an adverse effect on the growth of aquarium plants.

184. Algae Control: What can I do to control the algae in my aquarium?

You can wipe the algae off the aquarium glass and the fixtures with a sponge. Plants are more difficult to clean. Remove filamentous algae by twirling it around a small stick. In general, make sure you provide optimal water quality with low levels of nitrate and phosphate. This way you will prevent unwanted algae from growing in your tank. In addition, you can switch off the light for a few hours or even leave the tank in the dark for several days. This will inhibit the growth of algae. Another measure would be to introduce algae-eating fish, especially some of the live-bearing toothcarps or catfish, although aquarists generally expect too much of catfish as a method for getting rid of algae. Pet stores carry a number of products for controlling algae. However, this is only a cosmetic treatment of the problem. The success is short-lived because it does not remove the underlying cause of algae growth. Caution: Products containing copper can harm snails and plants in your aquarium. Peat is also an option for reducing algae growth. It softens the water, so you can use this method only if you are keeping soft-water fish in your tank.

185. Algae Species: A friend told me about various types of algae. Are there really different species?

Your friend is right. There are different species of algae, which can be classified as follows.

➤ Diatoms: They are usually brown in color, and their growth is favored primarily by high levels of silicate in the water.

➤ Brush algae: These are tufted green algae that occur especially when nitrate and phosphorus levels are too high.

➤ Filamentous algae: Filamentous green algae indicate good water quality.

➤ Green algae: Green growths on aquarium glass, driftwood, and rocks develop when lighting conditions are good or when sunlight hits the tank.

➤ Blue-green algae: They are not just blue but come in a variety of other colors as well. These organisms are actually cyanobacteria. Also known as slime algae, they can quickly cover plants, aquarium glass, and decorations with a slimy film. They have a strong musty or moldy odor and always show up in heavily polluted water.

EXTRA TIP

Barley straw for algae control
You can use barley straw to control algae successfully and without harmful side effects. It inhibits the growth of algae. For a tank with a volume of about 25 gallons (100 L), you need a handful of well-dried barley straw. Put the straw into a nylon stocking, and hang it in the tank. When the algae have cleared up, remove the straw and then carry out a partial water change (about 50 percent of the water in the tank).

186. Ammonia: Why is ammonia harmful for aquarium fish?

Ammonia (NH_3) is a waste by-product of fish metabolism. It is extremely toxic to cells and is almost always fatal for fish at concentrations greater than 1 ppm. However, even levels above 0.05 ppm cause chronic poisoning and can be fatal for fish that are sensitive or have already been weakened. You can determine the ammonia level with tests from the pet store. Signs of poisoning in the fish can be abnormal swimming behavior, excessive agitation, and refusal to eat. However, ammonia forms only at a pH above 7. If the water is acidic (pH below 7), ammonium (NH_4^+) is present, and this is not harmful to fish.

187. Buying Live Foods: Where can I get live foods for my fish?

You can buy live foods at the pet store. You can also culture some live foods yourself without much trouble—for example white worms, fruit flies, or vinegar eels.

Some aquarists collect live foods themselves. Earthworms from the garden, for example, are a real treat for larger predatory fish like cichlids. Others harvest microorganisms from ponds or puddles using fine-mesh nets. However, this could cause problems with the property owners, so make sure to get permission first.

Also, if you harvest live foods from pools or puddles, make certain that the water is clean. You should not feed your fish with food from polluted water, as this could make them sick or even kill them. You can easily raise mosquito larvae and water fleas yourself in a rain barrel during the summer months.

188. Care During Vacation: We are looking for someone to take care of our aquarium while we are on vacation. How can we find a suitable person?

If you are a member of an aquarium club, you can certainly find another club member to look after your aquarium during your absence. You can always return the favor when your tank sitter goes on vacation. If you are not a member of an aquarium club, then you can advertise in the local paper for someone to take care of your aquarium while you are away. Some animal shelters and humane societies may be able to recommend pet sitters. You can also contact the National Association of Professional Pet Sitters or Pet Sitters International. If necessary, you can always ask helpful family members or neighbors, but then be sure to give them detailed instructions.

189. Changing Hardness: How can I change the hardness of my water?

A variety of different techniques can be used to make hard water softer.
➤ You can use distilled water and mix it with tap water. However, this is recommended only for small quantities; otherwise, it gets to be too expensive.
➤ A better method is to use reverse osmosis water. To do this, you need a reverse osmosis unit that produces soft water from tap water. Water can also be softened with an ion exchange unit.
➤ You can use peat to soften the water and lower the pH at the same time. Put the peat into a media bag in the aquarium or directly into the filter. Peat releases humic acids into the water, which soften it. Alder cones (strobiles) work the same way. Be careful, though. The pH of very soft water is unstable, and it can undergo extreme fluctuations. This can become

life threatening for your fish. If your fish need hard water and the water in the aquarium is too soft, you can increase the hardness by adding calcareous rocks or clam shells to the tank.

190. Cleaning: Is it better to carry out just a partial water change or to clean the entire tank frequently?

For an aquarium in which everything is in order and the water parameters are in the green zone, you should never undertake a general cleaning.

Regularly carrying out a partial water change is sufficient. You have to clean the filter when necessary and occasionally vacuum up the debris from the substrate. However, if all the fish in your tank have died, you will have to clean the entire tank before you put in new fish. Discard any filter media and decorations that cannot be disinfected as well as all the plants.

191. Cleaning Decorations: Do I have to clean the decorations in my aquarium?

Normally the decorations do not need to be cleaned since a certain amount of algae growth should always be present. This is especially true if you have algae-eating fish in your tank like bristlenose catfish. However, the aquarium looks much tidier if at least some of the decorations are cleaned now and then. To do this, remove the decorations from the tank a few at a time and scrub them under lukewarm water.

A tip: Use this brush exclusively for your aquarium and never let it come into contact with chemical cleaners. The residue of any chemical substance could be transferred to the decorations and, thus, into the aquarium. Many chemical cleaners are highly toxic to fish, even in very small quantities.

192. Cleaning the Filter: **How often must I clean the filter?**

There are no set intervals for this chore. The filter should be cleaned when it is dirty. You can usually tell it is time when you notice a substantial decrease in filter output and the filter is producing just a weak trickle instead of a powerful stream. The intervals between cleanings can vary greatly.

You will usually have to clean an internal filter in a heavily stocked aquarium every 14 days. With a large external filter in a sparsely stocked and well-maintained tank, two to three months can pass before the filter has to be cleaned again. However, I suggest you check your filter every day to make sure it is running properly and the output is sufficient. This way there will not be any surprises, and you can integrate filter cleaning into your regular aquarium maintenance schedule.

193. Cleaning the Filter: **What must I pay attention to when I clean the filter?**

Open the filter canister, and remove the filter media. Rinse these under running water until no more dirt comes out. When you do this, the temperature of the tap water should match that of the aquarium water. Do not wash the filter media with hot water, or you will harm the filter bacteria. Never use soap or other cleaning products.

If you are replacing filter media, such as filter floss, you should remove only part of it at any one time so that it does not have to be completely recolonized by the filter bacteria.

Because the proper functioning of your filter is vital to the welfare of your fish, you should take great care in cleaning your filter. This is not a task that should be performed quickly or carelessly.

194. Cleaning the Glass: **How and how often do I clean the glass walls of my aquarium?**

You should clean both the inside and the outside of the glass once a week. To clean the inner surfaces, get an algae magnet at the pet store. You can use this practical device to clean the glass without getting your hands wet. You can also rub off the coating of algae with a sponge. Use a special scraper from the pet store to remove very stubborn films of algae and mineral deposits, but do not damage the silicone seal in the process. You can also put snails and algae-eating catfish into the tank to get rid of algae on the glass walls. However, they will remove the algae from only some areas. You always have to clean the front and side walls by hand so you can see into the tank clearly.

Clean the outside of the glass with a cloth and warm water. Do not use any chemical products like window cleaners. If some of it gets into the water, the cleaner could poison the fish.

195. Color in Goldfish: **Unfortunately, my goldfish are very pale. I have read that some foods are supposed to intensify their color. Does that really work?**

There are a variety of foods at the pet store that can actually intensify the color of Goldfish.

Goldfish varieties with different shapes and colors were already being bred in China 1,000 years ago.

However, this works only for shades of yellow, orange, and red. This food contains carotenoids, which are stored in the skin and musculature of the fish, intensifying the red shades.

196. Competition for Food: I have the impression that my fish snatch all the food away from the bottom-dwelling species before it reaches them. What can I do?

Since many bottom-dwelling fish like catfish are crepuscular (active at dusk or dawn) or nocturnal (active at night), you should feed them in the evening after you switch off the lights. Most fish are active during the daylight hours (diurnal) and are resting then. Use tablet foods, which sink rapidly to the bottom. If the bottom-dwelling fish still are not getting enough, you can also put food tablets into a cave.

197. Conductivity: I keep reading about the conductivity of the water. What does this mean?

You can use conductivity to estimate the total concentration of ions dissolved in the water. These ions can conduct electricity, which is the reason for the term conductivity. In freshwater, it is measured in µS/cm (µS = microSiemens). The more dissolved ions there are in the water, the higher the conductivity. Hard water always has a higher conductivity than soft water. A conductivity of 30 µS /cm corresponds to approximately 1° carbonate hardness. If the carbonate hardness is 10°, the conductivity is over 300 µS /cm. In aquarium water, conductivity should be between 250 and 900 µS /cm. As a rule, fish and aquatic plants have problems if the conductivity is either too low or too high. Adding table salt or medications to the aquarium water, increases the conductivity.

You can measure conductivity only with a special, relatively expensive device. Laboratories or well-equipped pet stores also have this sort of equipment. You can take a water sample there to have the conductivity determined, for example if you want to breed a fussy species for which the water parameters must be just right.

198. *Cryptocoryne:* **All the *Cryptocoryne* in my tank are dying. What is causing this?**

This is probably due to *Cryptocoryne* disease, also known as *Cryptocoryne* rot. It first manifests itself by the development of holes in the leaves or on the leaf margins. Starting at the tip, the leaf then becomes glassy and transparent and later disintegrates into a slimy mass. All the leaves and stems are affected. Usually the entire cryptocoryne population gets sick, while the other aquarium plants stay healthy. A variety of factors cause *Cryptocoryne* rot. Normally it is not an infection but, rather, a reaction of the plant to drastic changes in environmental conditions. This could be, for instance, due to replacement of the fluorescent bulbs or a severe deterioration of the water quality. *Cryptocoryne* species are especially intolerant of high phosphate levels due, for example, to overfertilization. Once

Remove all the decaying plant matter with a gravel vacuum, and then carry out a partial water change.

Cryptocoryne rot reaches the final stage, you should remove the decayed plant material with a gravel vacuum and then change 50 percent of the water. The roots usually grow back after a recovery period. In order to prevent this disease, never replace all the fluorescent bulbs at the same time, and be sure to check the water parameters regularly. Do not plant the individual *Cryptocoryne* too close to each other, and thin dense stands regularly.

199. Culturing Live Foods: Which live foods can I raise myself? How is it done?

➤ You can easily culture white worms or Grindal worms in a little box with some dirt.

➤ If you have a rain barrel in your yard, you can collect mosquito larvae. The females lay their eggs in the water, which then hatch into larvae.

➤ If you bury a tub in the garden and add a starter culture of water fleas, with a bit of luck you will be able to feed them to your fish throughout most of the year.

➤ You can raise fruit flies (*Drosophila*) in glass jars containing a mixture of yeast and fruit.

200. Daily Maintenance Chores: Which maintenance chores must I carry out daily?

You should always check the equipment and the fish at least once a day. Is the temperature correct? Are the filter, lights, and timer working properly? Fish are normally fed once a day. Observe your fish daily while they are eating. Are they behaving normally? This way you will become familiar with the behavior patterns of your fish and notice if problems have arisen. Paying insufficient attention to aquarium maintenance could lead to tragedy in your aquarium.

MAINTENANCE SCHEDULE
FOR AQUARIUM PLANTS

Daily	➤ Check plants ➤ Check lighting, temperature, and timer
Weekly	➤ Carry out partial water change ➤ Vacuum up debris from the substrate ➤ Remove dead and damaged leaves ➤ Fertilize if necessary ➤ Check water parameters
Monthly	➤ Cut back plants or thin out dense clumps
As needed	➤ Replant or fasten down plants drifting around in the water ➤ Replace fluorescent bulbs ➤ Fertilize plants (first determine iron level in water if necessary) ➤ Replace plants that are not growing

201. Disinfection: What is meant by disinfection, and when is it necessary?

Disinfection means killing germs like bacteria, viruses, and fungi. This be done by heating above 212°F (100°C) or using certain disinfectants. Disinfection is necessary only when you have to remove pathogens from objects. The objects must be cleaned thoroughly beforehand, or the disinfectant will not work. The best thing you can use for disinfecting objects is a disinfectant from the pharmacy. Special disinfectants for fish ponds are also available that are suitable for aquarium use. You must rinse objects well after disinfecting them, because fish can be very sensitive to chemical residues.

202. Duckweed: **The entire surface of my aquarium is covered by duckweed. What can I do to remedy this?**

The simplest method is to fish out the duckweed regularly with a net. Replacing your fluorescent bulbs with some that have a different light spectrum might also help. You could also harden the water in order to inhibit the growth of duckweed since it likes rather soft and slightly acidic water. Keep in mind, though, that this makes sense only if you have fish that prefer hard water, such as Boeseman's Rainbow-fish (*Melanotaenia boesemani*)—which, by the way, actively eat duckweed.

203. Electricity and Water: **Why should I unplug all equipment before working in the tank?**

The combination of electricity and water is always dangerous. Be sure to unplug everything before you work in the aquarium. If, for example, the water level drops too low during a water change, the heater can overheat and even shatter. This can electrify the water. The fish would probably not survive. If you were working in the tank at the time, you would be in danger as well.

204. Feeding: **What is the correct way to feed my fish?**

Commercial dry foods provide a good basic diet for most aquarium fish. Of course, you should still treat your fish to frozen or live foods as often as possible. You can also give plant-eating species like bristlenose catfish fresh vegetables now and then—for example, a slice of cucumber. The fish can digest these green foods better if you pour boiling water over the vegetables first or heat the vegetables in the micro-wave oven for a few seconds on high.

If you are unsure about what types of food to feed the species in your aquarium, you should consult an expert, such as an aquarium store owner. That individual should be able to give you guidance about what foods are most appropriate for your fish.

205. Feeding Baby Fish: How should I feed my baby fish, and what must I keep in mind?

When feeding your baby fish (fry), you must pay special attention to the size of the fish.

➤ Relatively large fry, such as Guppies, Platies, or Swordtails, can be fed with finely ground dry foods or powdered food (from the pet store).

➤ Fry that hatch from eggs are still usually too small for powdered food like this. Feed them the newly hatched larvae, or "nauplii", of brine shrimp (*Artemia*), which you can culture yourself. These are also known as baby brine shrimp.

➤ Even these are too large for really tiny fry. You should feed them protozoa that you can raise from

EXTRA TIP

Culturing live foods

If you are keeping very small fish species in your aquarium or regularly raise baby fish, you should culture vinegar eels. It is not difficult and does not require much space. Put a layer of oatmeal about 1/2 inch (1 cm) deep into a small plastic box with a lid. Wet it well, add the starter culture of vinegar eels (from the pet store). Keep it constantly moist. Before long, you will have plenty of the little worms, and then you can feed them to your fish.

granules (available at the pet store) or in a hay infusion. To do this, put a handful of hay into an empty jelly jar and pour water over it. Let the jar stand in a warm room for three to seven days, and the hay infusion will be ready.

➤ Feed your fry several times a day.

➤ Watch your fry closely to make sure that they are not getting too much or too little to eat. A proper diet will ensure that they grow up to be healthy adults.

206. Feeding Beef Heart: Lately I have been feeding my fish exclusively with beef heart because they like it so much. Does this provide adequate nutrition?

No, because beef heart does not contain enough dietary fiber. In the long run, this can lead to digestive problems, especially in fish that eat everything (omnivores). Furthermore, beef heart contains considerably more phosphorus than calcium. A calcium deficiency can have an adverse effect on the skeleton. For example, it can cause curvature of the spine. You should always avoid an unbalanced diet, regardless of what you feed. Like people, fish do best when they receive the full range of nutrients from a balanced diet.

Sterba's Cory (Corydoras sterbai) *eats insect larvae, worms, and other tiny creatures.*

207. Feeding Behavior: What do fish actually eat in the wild?

Fish in the wild have an extremely varied diet. Some fish eat plants (herbivores), some eat meat (carnivores), and some eat everything and anything (omnivores). Most fish are omnivores, and their diet can consist of plants as well as animals. Depending on the size of the fish, they can prey on anything from unicellular organisms to aquatic insects and their larvae. Larger predatory fish eat smaller fish, mammals, and even birds.

208. Feeding Guidelines: Are there guidelines that I should follow when feeding my fish?

Take your time when feeding your fish. Watch to see if all the fish can get at the food and if they are all eating. I suggest you observe the following guidelines for feeding your fish.

➤ Once a day, feed your fish as much as they can polish off in three minutes. Uneaten food should never be left in the water since this can make the water quality deteriorate so badly that the fish suffer as a result.

EXTRA TIP

Automatic feeder
If you are frequently away from home for a few days, you can get an automatic feeder. One model has a small container with a door. It attaches to the aquarium in such a way that flakes or granules of food drop into the tank when this door opens. You can use a timer to control when and for how long the door opens. The longer it stays open, the more food gets into the tank.

WHICH FOOD FOR WHICH FISH?

Small juveniles and fry	➤ Infusoria from hay infusion or commercial granules ➤ Baby brine shrimp (*Artemia* nauplii) ➤ Hard-boiled, finely mashed egg yolks
Juvenile fish (¼–½ inch/ 5–15 mm)	➤ Baby brine shrimp (*Artemia* nauplii) ➤ Vinegar eels, microworms ➤ Finely powdered food (dry food)
Small ornamental fish (½–1½ inch/ 1.5–4 cm)	➤ Dry food as flakes or granules ➤ Water fleas and copepods ➤ Mosquito larvae and glassworms
Medium-size ornamental fish (1½–2¾ inch/ 4–7 cm)	➤ Dry food as flakes or granules ➤ Water fleas ➤ Bloodworms, glassworms, and mosquito larvae ➤ Tubifex worms ➤ White worms ➤ Amphipods (*Gammarus*)
Large ornamental fish (larger than 2¾ inches/ 7 cm)	➤ Dry food as flakes, pellets, or sticks ➤ Tubifex worms ➤ Amphipods (*Gammarus*) ➤ Earthworms (minced if necessary) ➤ White worms ➤ Small feeder fish
Surface-swimming fish	➤ Dry food as flakes ➤ Fruit flies and springtails ➤ Live and frozen foods
Bottom-dwelling fish	➤ Dry food as tablets or granules ➤ Live or frozen foods appropriate for their size ➤ Plant-eating fish: lettuce, thin slices of cucumber, potatoes, and other vegetables

➤ Choose food that is the right size and type for your species. Give bottom-dwelling fish tablet foods that sink quickly to the bottom.

➤ Feed at the right time. Many catfish and other bottom-dwelling or secretive species are nocturnal and should be fed in the evening after the lights have been turned off. If you feed during the day, the other fish are usually much faster, so that the nocturnal fish lose out.

➤ Do not put the food into a feeding ring, because sometimes the dominant fish monopolize the feeding area. Small and subordinate fish cannot get to the food and go hungry.

➤ Do not give your fish just dry food all the time, but vary their diet as much as possible. At least once a week, give them frozen or live foods. Plant-eating species also enjoy fresh vegetables.

209. Feeding Habits: How do I know in which water level my fish prefer to feed?

You can tell the feeding habits of a fish if you look at its mouth.

In fish that find their food at the water surface, the lower jaw is longer than the upper jaw and the cleft of the mouth is turned upward. This way they can capture insects and other prey floating on top of the water.

In fish that feed on the bottom, the cleft of the mouth is turned downward and the upper jaw is longer than the lower jaw.

The mouth is often horizontal in fish that feed in midwater. Upper and lower jaws are of equal length.

Algae-eating catfish usually have a sort of sucker mouth in which the upper jaw is longer than the lower jaw.

If your tank contains bottom feeders as well as fish that feed at higher water levels, make sure that sufficient amounts of food filter down to the lower levels. You do not want bottom feeders to suffer from malnutrition.

210. Feeding in the Pond: **We have four Goldfish that spend the summer in a very small pond (about 20 gallons [80 L]). Should I give them supplemental food?**

With a small pond like this, you should give them supplemental food. The modest amount of algae and the few insects that fall into the water are not enough to feed the fish.

A larger pond, which contains an abundance of insects and their larvae as well as plant food like algae, is different. In this case, the fish will get fat if they are regularly fed dry food. Of course, you must observe the fish in a larger pond to make certain that they are getting enough food to eat. If it turns out that they are not, then you will need to supplement their diet with dry food.

211. Feeding Mistakes: **Why does overfeeding harm the fish?**

If fish are fed too much, they become obese and often develop a fatty liver. As a result, the liver can no longer perform its function and the fish die. In addition, fish that are overfed produce more feces and urine. That fouls the water in the aquarium, which in turn has an adverse effect on the health of the fish. Additionally, if too much uneaten food remains in the water, it begins to decay, which leads to the formation of hydrogen sulfide. If you do not intervene, this can become life threatening for your fish.

212. Fertilizing Plants: **Why is fertilizing plants with carbon dioxide a good idea?**

Carbon dioxide (CO_2) is a gas that plants require for growth along with heat, light, and nutrients. It is given off by the fish during respiration. However, in a heavily planted tank, the amount of carbon dioxide produced by the fish is usually not sufficient for optimal plant growth. A carbon dioxide deficiency can be one reason why aquarium plants do not grow properly. If you can rule out other factors, such as inadequate lighting, as the cause of poor plant growth, then you should provide supplemental carbon dioxide fertilization. Another course of action would be to add more fish to the aquarium. You should only consider this course of action if the size of your tank permits. Finally, you could remove some of the plants so that there is more CO_2 left for the remaining ones.

213. Fertilizing Plants: What must I keep in mind if I want to fertilize with carbon dioxide?

Make sure that the optimal baseline concentration of carbon dioxide is between 5 and 15 ppm. Higher concentrations over extended periods can be harmful for the fish. At night when there is no light, plants stop photosynthesizing, and carbon dioxide is no longer broken down. That is when the carbon dioxide level can rise too high. To prevent this, you should provide supplemental aeration of the aquarium at night using a timer and limit carbon dioxide fertilization to the daylight hours.

Remember, carbon dioxide is not present in water as a gas but is dissolved as an acid. That is why carbon dioxide fertilization changes the pH of the aquarium water, so be sure to check the pH regularly.

214. Flake Foods: How long can I use flake food after opening the container?

You should use a container of flake food within three months after opening it. This is why you should buy only small containers of flake food for small and medium-size aquariums. You should figure out how much food you will need over a three-month period and buy just that much.

215. Flake Foods: How should I store dry food so that it stays fresh?

Always reseal a container of dry food tightly after opening it, and store it in a cool, dry place. Dry food absorbs water and can become contaminated with molds after a while. These form toxic substances called aflatoxins, which may cause fatal liver damage in fish. You should never put the dry food container on the aquarium hood—the temperature is too warm there. Do not use dry food after its expiration date, because then the vitamin content is greatly reduced.

216. Floating Plants: I used to have beautiful floating plants in my tank, but now they are all dying. What could be responsible?

Perhaps the quality of light in the aquarium has deteriorated. This is frequently the cause when floating plants grow poorly or die. In this case, replace the fluorescent bulbs so the floating plants will thrive again. You should also check the water parameters. Many floating plants prefer soft, slightly acidic water and do poorly in hard, alkaline water. Perhaps you have installed a new filter that is producing a stronger current. Most floating

Carbon dioxide fertilization ensures good growth of aquarium plants, like this cryptocoryne.

plants cannot tolerate a strong flow, and that could be the cause of your problem.

217. Frozen Foods: What are frozen foods, and where do I get them?

Frozen foods are an alternative to live foods for carnivorous and omnivorous fish. The advantage of frozen foods is that they can always be kept on hand. They consist of live foods that are frozen in small portions immediately after capture. Bloodworms, mosquito larvae, glassworms, water fleas, and *Mysis* (freshwater shrimp) as well as beef heart mixtures are available in frozen form. You can get frozen foods in the pet store, where different varieties are sold in flat packs or trays of minicubes.

218. Gas Bubbles: All of a sudden, gas bubbles are rising from the substrate of our aquarium. What does that mean, and what should I do?

Pockets of decay may have formed in the substrate and be releasing hydrogen sulfide, which is toxic for fish. If so, then there will be an odor of rotten eggs. In this case, you have to move the fish and vacuum up the detritus.

The entire substrate could also be covered by a carpet of green algae, in which case these bubbles are just oxygen given off by the algae, which is even beneficial for the fish. Naturally, you do not have to do anything if this is the case.

219. Handling Fish: Is it true that you should not touch fish unless your hands are wet?

Yes, that is true. The surface of the fish's body is covered with a thin layer of mucus. It reduces frictional resist-

ance when the fish swims and contains active substances that protect the fish against bacteria and fungi.
With wet hands or, better yet, moistened disposable
(latex) gloves, you will not damage the slime coat over
the fish's scales. If your hands are dry, you could remove
part of this slime coat. Then harmful bacteria and fungi
could settle on the fish's skin and cause disease. However, it is always better to remove your fish from the
tank with a fish net instead of with your hands.

**220. Hardness: What exactly is meant by total
hardness?**

Water contains calcium and magnesium salts, primarily in the form of carbonates and sulfates. Other salts
are also present, although they are less important for
measuring water hardness. Aquarists distinguish
between carbonate hardness (also called temporary
hardness), which is determined by the concentration
of carbonate ions, and permanent hardness, which
depends on the concentration of sulfate ions and
other salt ions. Carbonate hardness and permanent
hardness together make up total hardness. This is
measured in °dGH (German degrees of hardness),
where 1°dGH equals 17.8 ppm calcium carbonate.
The more magnesium and calcium carbonates present
in a specific volume of water, the harder it is. Soft
water has a hardness of 0–7°dGH, moderately hard
water has 7–14°dGH, hard water has 14–21°dGH, and
very hard water has a hardness above 21°dGH.

**221. How Much to Feed: I am never sure if my fish
are getting enough food. How much food do
they actually need?**

Many aquarists mean well and overestimate the
amount of food their fish need. That is why aquarium
fish are frequently overfed. The fish get fat as a result.

If the pH is above 7, they can be poisoned by the ammonia resulting from too much organic waste.

The maintenance requirement for fully grown fish is about 1 percent of the body weight. Most aquarium fish weigh between 0.07 and 0.35 ounce (2 and 10 gm), which means they need only the minute amount of 0.0007–0.0035 ounce (0.02–0.1 gm) of dry food per fish per day. A good rule of thumb is to feed the fish once a day, giving them only as much food as they can eat in three minutes. Growing and breeding fish have a higher energy requirement, however, and for this reason must be fed more. The amount of food required by juvenile fish depends on their size, and they must be fed several times a day.

222. Hydras: A friend told me about a troublesome freshwater polyp (hydra). What is it exactly, and can it be controlled?

Freshwater polyps (hydras) are tiny coelenterates with tentacles. They can cause considerable damage in tanks with baby fish but are harmless for fish over 1/2 inch (1 cm) in length. Hydras reproduce especially well if you overfeed your fish with water fleas or other small invertebrates in the form of live or frozen foods. If you have an outbreak of hydras, cut back on these foods. Some fish, particularly Paradise Fish, devour these creatures

Freshwater polyps (hydras) can be especially dangerous to baby fish less than 1/2 inch (1 cm) in length.

and can rid your tank of the infestation. This works especially well if you feed your fish sparingly for a while. Hydras can also be killed by chemical products from the pet store or medications from the veterinarian. However, snails and other invertebrates are killed by these medications, too.

223. **Improving Water Quality: I measured all the water parameters and discovered that they are not in order. What should I do?**

That depends on which water parameters are not in order. Carry out a partial water change several days in a row. On the first day, change 30 percent of the water, then 20 percent a day on subsequent days, until the water values are once again within acceptable limits. Caution—never replace the water completely since fish have trouble tolerating any drastic change, even if it leads to better values.

If the water quality is good, Lemon Tetras are happy.

You should also check to see if your filter output is adequate or if the filter is dirty. If the problem lies here, then you will have to clean the filter or buy a new one. You could also install an additional filter.

Stop feeding your fish entirely for two to three days, and afterwards give them only as much food as they can polish off in three minutes. There should never be any leftover food. A few days without food will not harm full-grown fish in the least.

224. Live Foods: What can I give my fish as live foods?

If you do not want to breed feeder animals yourself, you will find a large assortment of live foods at well-stocked pet supply stores. For smaller fish, you can use water fleas, copepods, brine shrimp, vinegar eels, glassworms, and mosquito larvae. Suitable foods for medium-sized fish, in addition to those just mentioned, are tubifex worms, white worms, and bloodworms. Larger fish readily accept earthworms and small feeder fish. For fish that swim at the water surface, such as Redchin Panchax, halfbeaks, and hatchetfish, you can also feed small insects like fruit flies.

225. Live Foods: Are any problems associated with feeding live foods?

As a rule, live foods are recommended for carnivorous and omnivorous fish. However, it depends on where you get them. Pathogens like bacteria or fish parasites can be introduced into the aquarium along with live foods. That is why you should never collect food organisms in waters where fish are also found. Live foods can also harbor predatory creatures that will not hesitate to attack fry or small fish. Freshwater polyps (hydras) are one such danger to the aquarium.

Some of the favorite live foods, especially tubifex worms and bloodworms, are usually found in heavily polluted waters. In that case, they will be contaminated with pollutants, such as heavy metals. For this reason, I suggest that you either culture live foods yourself or buy them at the pet store.

226. Loss of Appetite: Some of the fish in my aquarium are not eating well. What causes that?

If your fish are eating poorly or not at all, something is wrong. Check to see if any of the following are responsible.

➤ You are giving them the wrong food. Specialized feeders, for example, need special food.

➤ The water temperature is too low.

➤ Other water parameters are not in order, for example pH or oxygen, nitrite, or ammonia levels.

➤ These are subordinate fish that are being kept away from their food by a dominant fish.

If all the aquarium conditions are in order and the fish have been eating well up to now, this is probably due to a disease. However, refusal to eat is only a very general disease sign. It does not explain the nature or cause of the disease. The best thing to do in a case like this is ask a veterinarian for advice.

227. Mineral Deposits: How do I get rid of mineral deposits on the aquarium glass?

The best way to remove mineral deposits (scale) is with a razor blade scraper, available from the pet store. You can then wipe off the residue with a soft cloth. Do not let it fall back into the tank, or it will just harden the water again. Metal scrubbing pads are not suitable. They can put fine scratches in the glass that can eventually lead to the formation of blind spots. Mineral deposits can also be removed using a pH-lowering product (available at the pet store). Put a little of this solution onto a cotton ball or a small sponge, and scrub the affected spot with it. Since these preparations are usually acids, you should wear gloves when using them so they do not irritate your skin. Never use household lime deposit removers, because many of these solvents are very toxic for fish. Besides, they can lower the pH drastically if they get into the aquarium water.

228. Nitrate Levels: I have measured a high nitrate level of 80 ppm in my tank. What does that mean, and what should I do about it?

A high level of nitrate (NO_3) means that the water is rather heavily loaded with organic matter. Nitrate itself is harmful to the fish only in relatively high concentrations. However, a comparison with the initial level is always necessary. The level for aquarium water should be at most 30 ppm above this initial value. This means that if your tap water has practically no nitrate and your aquarium water is at 80 ppm, aquarium hygiene is poor. On the other hand, if the tap water has a nitrate level of 50 ppm, then this value is still within the normal range. Nitrate levels above 150 ppm are harmful for the fish.

   If the nitrate level is high (over 50 ppm), you should immediately carry out a partial water change, possibly several days in a row. Discontinue feeding for one to two days, and then feed sparingly after that.

229. Nitrite Levels: What does a high nitrite level mean?

Nitrite (NO_2) is harmful for fish and can even cause death at a concentration of 0.1 ppm. An increase in nitrite could be due to overstocking, overfeeding, dead fish in the aquarium, or heavily polluted tap water. With nitrite poisoning, the fish hang at the water surface and breathe rapidly. Act quickly, and carry out a water change.

230. Overfeeding: Our child accidentally dumped an entire container of flake food into the aquarium. What should we do?

If the food is still floating on the surface, immediately skim it all off with a net. If it has already sunk to the bottom, vacuum it up with a hose. Do not postpone this task until the next day, because the excess food will have already begun to decay and the water quality will deteriorate.

231. Oxygen Level: How high should the oxygen level in the water be, and what is the correlation between oxygen level and temperature?

For most fish species, an oxygen level of 4–5 ppm is sufficient. However, fish that come from fast-flowing streams require a higher oxygen level (more than 5 ppm). If fish have a supplemental method of breathing, like labyrinth fish, they can even live in oxygen-deprived waters. The warmer the water, the less oxygen can be dissolved in it. The cooler the water, the more oxygen it usually holds.

232. pH: What is the relationship between pH and water hardness?

The pH indicates the acidity and thus the quality of the water. Soft water normally has a neutral to acidic pH, while hard water has a neutral to alkaline pH.

MAINTENANCE SCHEDULE
FOR THE AQUARIUM

Daily	➤ Feed the fish. ➤ Observe the fish closely: Are they all swimming and behaving normally? Are they all eating spontaneously? ➤ Check the equipment: heater, thermometer, filter, lights, timer. ➤ Check the plants. ➤ If necessary, remove dead fish immediately. ➤ When culturing live foods, make sure nothing is moldy or infested with mites. If necessary, add nutrient medium.
Weekly	➤ Water change: replace 20–30 percent of the water with fresh water. ➤ Clean the aquarium glass. ➤ Test water parameters (pH, nitrate, nitrite, ammonia, total hardness).
Every two weeks to monthly	➤ Vacuum up debris from the substrate.
As needed	➤ Gently clean the filter. ➤ Remove mineral deposits. ➤ Replace fluorescent bulbs. ➤ Thin plants. ➤ Clean decorations. ➤ Clean equipment. ➤ Carry out necessary repairs or have them done. ➤ When culturing live foods, begin a new culture before the old starter culture is exhausted.

➤ pH 0–5.0: Extremely acidic and therefore inhospitable for fish.

➤ pH 5.0–6.0: Very acidic, very few fish can tolerate it for any length of time.

➤ pH 6.0–6.9: Acidic and therefore suitable for some fish, for instance those from tropical black-water rivers.

➤ pH 7.0: Neutral.

➤ pH 6.6–7.4: Weakly acidic to weakly alkaline and thus suitable for keeping most aquarium fish.

➤ pH 7.5–8.5: Alkaline and thus suitable for fish from Lake Malawi and Lake Tanganyika.

➤ pH 8.5–14.0: Extremely alkaline and inhospitable for fish.

233. Planarians: Little worms are crawling around on the glass walls of my aquarium. Could these be planarians?

Planarians, also known as flatworms, are tiny worms a fraction of an inch (1 to several mm) long that crawl around on the aquarium glass and decorations but also swim freely in the water. They have two small eyespots, which can easily be seen under the magnifying glass. Planarians feed on decaying plant and animal tissues as well as on microorganisms and other

EXTRA TIP

Bait trap for planarians

If planarians (flatworms) multiply on a massive scale in your aquarium, I suggest that you put in bait traps. To do this, put little bits of meat into several small, thin plastic tubes and place the tubes into the aquarium. The meat will attract the worms. Make sure that the traps are designed in such a way that the fish cannot eat the bait from them. Empty the contents of these plastic tubes daily.

tiny aquatic creatures. They can present a danger to fry but are not harmful to full-grown fish. For many aquarists, they are an aesthetic problem.

If no eyespots are present, these could be aquatic oligochaete worms (naidids). They feed on detritus and are harmless even for juvenile fish.

234. Planarians: I have a problem with planarians in my aquarium. What can I do?

Planarians reproduce prolifically if uneaten food or other organic material is in the tank. Therefore, the first step is to remove their source of food by keeping your aquarium scrupulously clean. Some fish, especially Paradise Fish, devour planarians but only if nothing more appealing is available to eat.

You can also use chemical agents available from the veterinarian or pet shop. However, these products will not eliminate the very resistant eggs of the planarians, so you will have to treat the tank several times. The major disadvantage of this method is that snails and possibly plants might die, as well. To protect the fish, you can transfer them to another tank before using chemical treatments. Sometimes increasing the temperature to 95°F (35°C) for three days also helps control planarians. The fish must be moved to a temporary tank during this period.

235. Plants Are Thin and Faded: The stems of my plants are getting long and thin, and the leaves are pale. What is causing this?

Your aquarium plants are probably getting too little light. One reason could be that the water surface is covered by too many floating plants. Simply remove some of the floating plants.

Another reason could be that the light intensity is too low. Replace the fluorescent bulbs, or get an additional light source for the hood.

236. Plants Are Yellowish: **The leaves of my aquarium plants are yellowish or faded. What could cause this?**

If the water parameters and other conditions are in order, there could be a deficiency of the trace elements iron or manganese. You can easily remedy the situation with special iron fertilizers available at the pet store. Since iron deficiency is frequently a problem, many aquarists regularly add iron fertilizer to the tank as a preventive measure.

237. Plants with Holes: **The plants in our aquarium have holes. What causes this?**

You probably have a lot of snails in your aquarium. Some species like ramshorn snails and pond snails really love aquarium plants. However, other snail species that are primarily algae eaters will sometimes attack aquarium plants if not enough other food is available for them. In this case I suggest you drastically reduce the number of snails in your tank.

Other types of damage to the plants, like nibbled leaves or missing tips on fine-leaved plants, point to your fish as the culprits. All other abnormalities and growth disturbances, however, are signs of nutrient deficiency or the result of overfertilization with specific substances.

Before you take any remedial action, you should find out exactly what problem you have on your hands. There is no sense taking an action that does not solve the problem.

238. Poor Plant Growth: My plants are stunted and will not grow. What can I do?

If your plants are stunted and stop growing, you should check the following.

➤ Light intensity: The light intensity should be at least 2 watts per gallon (0.5 watt/L) of water. Smaller tanks up to 25 gallons (100 L) are often equipped with only one fluorescent bulb (20 watts). However, 50 watts would be necessary to ensure adequate plant growth. Have an electrician install a second fluorescent bulb or buy a hood with two fluorescent bulbs.

➤ Light quality: Plants need light primarily in the blue and red regions of the spectrum. Plant bulbs are available with a spectral output especially designed to encourage plant growth.

➤ Age of the fluorescent bulbs: As the fluorescent bulbs age, their light output declines sharply. That is why you should replace the fluorescent bulbs after 12 months at the latest.

➤ Iron level in the water: If your tap water does not contain much iron, there can be an iron deficiency in the aquarium water. This is easily remedied with iron fertilizer from the pet store.

➤ Fish population: Some fish nibble constantly at the aquarium plants and can do quite a bit of damage to them. In this case, only use large, robust plants with tough leaves.

EXTRA TIP

No wild plants!
Never take plants from the wild or from your garden pond. You could introduce pathogens like bacteria or parasites into the aquarium along with them. Sometimes these aquatic plants also harbor unwelcome guests, like eggs or larvae of water beetles or dragonflies, which can pose a danger to the fish.

➤ Water quality: Some aquarium plants, for example many swordplants like the *Echinodorus* species, do better in soft water and die if the water is too hard.
➤ Too little carbon dioxide in the water: In this case, fertilize with carbon dioxide.

239. Preventing Algae Growth: What can I do to avoid excessive growth of algae in my aquarium?

Make sure to avoid the following.
➤ Too much organic waste in the water: This can be due to a variety of factors, for example overfeeding or neglecting to remove decaying plant matter. Infrequent or inadequate water changes, a dirty filter, or too many fish also create favorable conditions for excessive algae growth.
➤ Elevated nitrate level: The level of nitrate in the aquarium water must be correct. Algae begin to proliferate at nitrate concentrations greater than 50 ppm. If the nitrate level in your tap water is too high, you can remedy that by demineralizing the water or by using reverse osmosis water.
➤ Overfertilizing: Perhaps you used too much aquarium plant fertilizer or a product containing too much nitrogen.
➤ Too much phosphorus: Sometimes the phosphate level in your tap water is too high. This can happen if you use a phosphate filter cartridge to prevent calcium deposits (scale) in your pipes.
➤ Too much or too little light: If the aquarium is located too close to a window, sunlight hitting the tank can cause proliferation of green algae. The light output of the bulbs in the hood may also be too low.
➤ Too few or no aquarium plants: Aquarium plants compete with algae for nutrients and help keep them in check.

240. Room Temperature Too Warm: My attic often gets very hot in the summer. Will that harm my fish?

Provide good air circulation in the room, and keep fish that like higher temperatures, for example Rams (*Mikrogeophagus ramirezi*), Siamese Fighting Fish (*Betta splendens*), or Sailfin Mollies (*Poecilia velifera*). However, if the water temperature is always above 84°F (29°C), your only option is to set up the aquarium in a cooler room.

241. Sick Fish as Food: May I feed sick or dead fish to predatory fish and pond turtles?

You should never dispose of sick or dead fish in an aquarium with pond turtles or carnivorous fish, because diseases can be transmitted this way. Pond turtles can contract tuberculosis, and other fish can be infected with bacteria, parasites, or viruses. Fish with an incurable disease should be euthanized.

242. Snail Infestation: What can I do to control an infestation of snails in my aquarium?

There are several methods for controlling snail infestations in the aquarium.
➤ The simplest method is to gather and remove them conscientiously. This is easiest if you put some bait, for instance a slice of carrot or potato, into the aquarium in the evening. Remove it the next morning along with any snails still clinging to it.
➤ Alternatively, you can put in fish that will devour snail eggs and young snails—for example, Clown Loaches.

➤ The pet store carries products that will kill snails. However, the water will be seriously fouled if all the snails in the aquarium die at the same time. This high level of contamination could be fatal to the fish. In order to keep the snail problem from arising in the first place, you should feed your fish only as much as they will actually eat. After all, leftover food stimulates the reproductive activities of the snails.

> *The Molly* (Poecilia sphenops *var.*) *prefers to feed on algae and the microorganisms that live on it.*

243. Snails: My aquarium is overrun with snails, although I never added any. How did they get in?

You probably introduced the snails into your aquarium as eggs attached to aquarium plants. That is why you should examine new aquarium plants carefully and rinse them off under running water before you put them into your tank.

244. Specialized Feeders: Are some fish specialized feeders?

Yes, many fish need a very specific diet. Marine fish, in particular, include quite a few specialized feeders like the seahorse, which eats only tiny crustaceans. However, most aquarium fish do well on a diet of dry foods. Some labyrinth fish and killifish will refuse to eat dry foods, though, and then you have to give them live or frozen foods.

245. Substrate Fouling: The substrate in my tanks is fouling the water. What can I do?

Because organic decomposition generates hydrogen sulfide, which can be fatal for fish, you must take immediate corrective measures. You can recognize hydrogen sulfide because it smells like rotten eggs. First, transfer the fish to another tank so that they are not poisoned. Then carefully stir up the substrate at the affected spots and immediately vacuum up the debris (mulm) with a hose. In addition, you can improve the aeration of the water by positioning the filter outlet above the water surface and installing an airstone driven by a diaphragm pump. In the future, do not allow excess organic material to accumulate in the substrate.

In the wild, the Penang Betta (Betta pugnax) prefers to dine on insects that have fallen into the water.

1

Sardine cichlids (Cyprichromis and Paracyprichromis) feed exclusively on zooplankton in their natural habitat.

2

Decay often sets in when the substrate is too fine-grained. Here you can remedy the situation by mixing in some coarser sand. This way you will improve the aeration of the substrate. You can also put in trumpet snails, which are primarily bottom dwellers and rid the substrate of excess organic matter. Trumpet snails also loosen up the substrate by their movements. Last but not least, fish that dig around in the substrate looking for food can prevent fouling.

246. Time Allowances: How much time should I allow for taking care of the aquarium?

Routine tasks should take only a few minutes per day. Depending on the size and location of your tank, you will have to allow 15–40 minutes for weekly water changes. Little chores like cleaning the aquarium glass, pruning the plants, and replacing the fluorescent bulbs must be done as needed. In addition, you must also allow time for cleaning the filter, which will take about 20–60 minutes, depending on the type of filter (internal or external) and accessories in your tank. How often it has to be done varies from tank to tank.

247. Toxic Substances: Which toxic substances should I monitor regularly in the water?

Test the levels of nitrate, nitrite, ammonia, and phosphate regularly. The maximum levels are usually indicated on the test strips or the reagents (from the pet store). It is very important to watch the levels of these toxic substances. If they grow too high, they could cause serious illness or death. You should get into the habit of monitoring the levels of these substances according to a set schedule.

248. Vacation: We want to take a two-week trip. What should we keep in mind for the time we are away?

➤ You should not add any new fish, plants, or snails to your aquarium for at least 14 days before your scheduled vacation. This way, you will not introduce any diseases that you cannot monitor.

➤ Before your vacation, carry out a partial water change, and check all equipment carefully to make sure everything is working properly.

➤ If someone is taking care of your fish during your absence, explain to this person exactly how much food to give the fish. If the fish are overfed, they'll get sick and could even die as a result of all the organic waste in the water. If you are taking only a short vacation, do not have your substitute caretaker feed the fish.

➤ If you are going away for a longer period, you can use an automatic feeder. Alternatively, you can prepare little packets containing daily portions of food. This way you can be relatively certain that the pet sitter will feed your fish the correct foods in the correct amounts.

➤ Leave behind your address as well as the address of your pet shop in case of emergency.

249. Vegetarian Diet: My fish need a vegetarian diet. What can I feed them?

Green algae as well as blanched lettuce leaves, cucumber slices, peas, slices of potato, nettles, and other herbs are all suitable for plant-eating fish or omnivores that enjoy vegetable foods. As an alternative or a supplement, you can also feed plant-based flake and tablet foods, for example those having spirulina algae as the main ingredient.

250. Water: Can I use spring water, well water, or rain water for an aquarium?

In principle, you can use well water for an aquarium. However, you should first have the water tested by the proper authorities to see that the water parameters are suitable. Spring water can be used only if no fish are in the spring. Since almost 100 percent of wild fish carry parasites, introducing diseases into the aquarium is easy this way. Rain water can be used if it is uncontaminated and you need soft water.

251. Water Changes: What must I keep in mind when I want to change the water in my aquarium?

I definitely recommend that you carry out regular partial water changes. If you do not, then at some point the fish will be swimming in a soup of feces and urine. In principle, you should change about 20–30 percent of the water once a week. To do this, you need a hose and two or more buckets. First, fill the hose with water at the faucet, making sure that no air is in the hose, and then close both ends with your thumbs. Now hold one end of the hose in the aquarium water and the other in the bucket, making sure the bucket is lower than the aquarium. First open the end of the hose in the aquarium and then the other end in the bucket. The water will begin to flow. Stop the flow of water by using your thumb to close the end of the hose in the bucket. Make sure not to siphon up any fish. Never suck on the hose to start the water flowing. If you inadvertently swallow aquarium water, you could contract bacterial infections. The pet store even sells hoses equipped with a siphon starter.

Once you have removed the appropriate amount of water, refill the aquarium with tap water. The temperature of the fresh water should not vary too much from that of the water in the tank ($\pm4°F/2°C$). Fish are very sensitive to temperature and could suffer from temperature shock. In addition, make sure the water has the same pH and hardness as the water in the tank. You might have to condition your tap water beforehand. If the tap water contains chlorine, which is harmful for fish, you should either add a water conditioner (from the pet store) or allow the water to stand for a few hours in tubs so that the chlorine can escape. Ask your local water authority about the parameters of your tap water.

Many water systems now use chloramines. These will not dissipate by letting the water stand. Chemical removal is needed.

252. Water Cloudy: The water in our aquarium has suddenly become cloudy, and our fish are hanging at the water surface gasping for air. What should we do?

When unicellular microorganisms like ciliates and paramecia multiply drastically, the water becomes cloudy. An explosive increase in the population is only possible, though, if too much organic material is in the water, for example leftover food and dead plant matter. First remove this material. Then carry out a partial water change (about 50 percent), slowly adding the new water over one to two hours so that the fish get used to the change in water quality. You should not feed the fish for one to two days after that. Use an additional filter to keep the water moving vigorously. Installing a UV clarifier brings only temporary relief, because it does not remove the cause of the problem. In case you do not have fish in your aquarium yet, you can add water fleas, which feed on these microorganisms and thus filter the water.

253. Water Discolored: **The water in our new aquarium has turned brown. What can cause that and is it harmful?**

This could be due to a piece of bogwood that contains a lot of humic acids. These tannins and dyes are not harmful, but they stain the water yellow or brown. If your fish prefer a slightly acidic pH, you can leave the root in the tank without a second thought. If you change the water regularly, the discoloration of the water will eventually fade away on its own. In the future, soak bogwood for three weeks before you put it into the tank.

254. Water Parameters: **How can I measure the different water parameters in my aquarium?**

Electronic devices will allow you to measure pH and conductivity very precisely. However, you can also measure pH with test strips or liquid test kits from the pet store or pharmacy. These kits use a color scale that allows you to determine the pH fairly accurately.

The pet store also carries liquid test kits to measure levels of nitrate, nitrite, ammonia, and oxygen as well as hardness. You can determine the levels in a matter of minutes with these tests.

Water samples can also be tested at a pet store or laboratory.

255. Water Quality: How do I make sure that the water quality in my tank remains consistently good?

If you observe the following guidelines conscientiously, you'll have no problems.

➤ Stocking level: It should be appropriate for the size of the tank. The amount of feces and urine excreted by the fish will then be manageable.

➤ Filter performance: Choose a filter that is appropriate for the tank size and stocking level and that offers a suitable level of performance. Clean the filter regularly.

➤ Water changes: Carry out partial water changes conscientiously once a week.

➤ Feeding: Feed your fish the proper amount, not too much and not too little. Uneaten food fouls the water unnecessarily.

➤ Planting: Dense planting helps to maintain good water quality.

➤ Medications: Administer medications only when necessary. Antibiotics are especially harmful to filter bacteria and can cause a dramatic increase in nitrate and ammonia levels.

It cannot be stressed enough that maintaining good water quality is absolutely vital to maintaining a healthy aquarium. If you allow toxic substances to foul your aquarium, the health of your fish will certainly suffer, and they could even die.

256. Water Softening: **I would like to keep discus in my 250-gallon (1,000 L) tank, but I have very hard tap water. How can I get soft water in large quantities?**

A reverse osmosis unit is advisable here. The process known as reverse osmosis removes up to 98 percent of all dissolved substances from the water. In simple terms, the water is pressed through a special filter that holds back the dissolved substances. The less calcium and magnesium present in the water, the softer it is. Reverse osmosis units for softening the water are attached to the faucet. However, the water then has so little salt that you have to mix it with some of the tap water before you can use it for your aquarium. The mixing ratio depends on the hardness of the tap water and the desired hardness of the aquarium water. In your case, mix about 200 gallons (800 L) of reverse osmosis water with 50 gallons (200 L) of tap water.

257. Weekly Maintenance Chores: **Which maintenance chores must I carry out weekly?**

Once a week, you should change 20–30 percent of the water. Do not exceed this amount, though, or you will alter the water quality too drastically. To change the water, suction up the old water with a hose and replace it with fresh water. If your tap water is chlorinated, you should let it stand for a while in a tub. This permits the evaporation of chlorine gas, which is harmful for fish. I also recommend that you treat the fresh water with a commercial water conditioner that binds chlorine or harmful heavy metal ions.

Recognizing and Treating Diseases

If you know your fish and observe them closely every day, you will be sure to notice any signs of disease. In the following pages, you will find answers to the most frequent questions about prevention and treatment of diseases in fish.

258. Anesthesia and Surgery: Can fish actually be anesthetized and undergo surgery?

Fish can be anesthetized with a variety of anesthetic agents. To do this, the affected animal is removed from the aquarium and put into a spare tank.

The veterinarian usually adds the anesthetic directly to the water. Only in rare cases, for example with very large fish, is the anesthetic applied directly to the gills or administered by injection.

Anesthetics are necessary to tranquilize a fish for special tests like X-ray or ultrasound. They are absolutely essential for painful procedures like surgery. However, surgery is usually performed only on large, valuable fish like Koi, some cichlids, or Goldfish.

259. Broad-spectrum Medications: My fish are not eating, they are holding their fins close to their body, and they are shimmying. Would a broad-spectrum medication help?

Even if the name broad-spectrum medication suggests that it can be used to treat several diseases at once, these products are usually active against just one pathogen or a specific group of pathogens, for example unicellular external parasites. Even many prescription antibiotics are useful against only certain bacteria, while they are ineffective against others. If no precise diagnosis has been made by an expert, then choosing the correct effective medication is a gamble. The probability of picking the wrong one is very high. Since any medication has side effects that can cause further harm to the fish, you should not use any without a diagnosis. It is better to consult a veterinarian or your pet shop right away and get the correct medication.

260. Bubbles on the Eyes: After a major water change, my Angelfish developed a sort of bubble over its left eye. What is that, and how can I help the fish?

Your fish probably has gas bubble disease. This is comparable to decompression sickness (the bends) in humans and is caused by the water being supersaturated with gas. Tap water is often saturated with oxygen under high pressure to prevent corrosion of the pipes. When you are changing the water, if you introduce the water directly into the aquarium through a hose, the gas has no way of escaping before the tap water mixes with the aquarium water. Supersaturation with gas causes the fish to develop bubbles on its head and body, which look as if they were filled with clear fluid. The eyes are sometimes affected as well, and then they bulge (pop eye).

If the fish is eating and swimming normally, there is a relatively good chance that the bubbles will clear up on their own. However, if the fish's movements are uncoordinated or it lies on the bottom of the tank or on its side, then chances of recovery are slim. In this case, you should euthanize it.

EXTRA TIP

Preventing gas bubble disease

You can prevent gas bubble disease by letting the tap water flow into the aquarium through a spray attachment placed above the water surface. This way the gas can escape before the tap water mixes with the aquarium water. Alternatively, you can let the fresh tap water stand in a tub for a few hours before changing the water. This will allow the gas to escape along with chlorine, which is harmful to fish and is frequently dissolved in the water as well.

261. Color Changes: Three months ago, I added four young Goldfish to my 15-gallon (60 L) tank. Since then, the appearance of the fish has changed. Two of them have lost some of their black coloration. Could they be sick?

Your fish are not sick. It is normal for young Goldfish to change color over time. As juveniles they are all dark. As time passes, they take on their final coloration, which differs from one individual to the next. Typically, the back and belly are the last to change color. Consequently, a fish that was speckled when young will eventually be uniformly yellow, orange, or red. As you can see, there is no cause for concern.

262. Cottony Growths on the Skin: My fish have cottony growths on the skin and fins. What could this be?

These cottony growths, which frequently develop on the edges of the fins, around the mouth, or on wounds, are usually fungi. They cannot infect warm-

EXTRA TIP

Testing the water

If you notice changes in the social, eating, or swimming behavior of your fish, or if you see other signs of disease, the first thing you should do is test the individual water parameters. Are the concentrations of harmful compounds like nitrate, nitrite, and ammonia too high? If the levels are not within safe limits, you should take immediate steps to improve the water quality. However, if the parameters are in order, you should ask your veterinarian or pet shop to determine the cause of the problem.

blooded animals or humans. They are known as water molds and in most cases belong to the genus *Saprolegnia*. Fungi normally infect weakened fish that are already suffering from another disease or have been injured. You should have the underlying disease diagnosed and treated by the veterinarian or your pet shop.

In order to control the fungal infection directly, you can add an antifungal medication like malachite green or methylene blue to the water. However, that will not help in the long term if the underlying cause of the fungal growth is not removed. Discuss treatment options with your veterinarian or your pet shop.

263. Determining Cause of Death: Can I have a dead fish examined to find out if it had an infectious disease?

There are special diagnostic laboratories that examine dead fish. You can find the addresses on the Internet or inquire at your state or local veterinary medical society. However, you must have the fish examined as soon as possible, which means you must refrigerate it and take it to the laboratory within three hours of death. This is because most unicellular parasites become difficult or impossible to identify even just a few hours after their host dies. In a small creature like a fish, pathological changes in the organs soon become impossible to evaluate, because decomposition sets in very quickly. There is no point in carrying out microbiological tests if the fish is in an advanced state of decay. Never send dead fish through the mail, because that will definitely take too long.

If you think that one of your fish has died from disease, it may be worth the effort to find out for certain, as you may be able to prevent further deaths in your aquarium.

It is much better to take a sick fish to the pet shop before it dies. Then the fish can be evaluated and euthanized if necessary. Afterward the pet shop can carry out the appropriate tests and initiate treatment to save the lives of the remaining aquarium fish.

264. Diagnosing Diseases: Which tests can a veterinarian perform if I want to know exactly what disease my fish have?

The veterinarian can take a skin smear and a gill smear and examine these under the microscope. This is especially useful for identifying external parasites, many of which are not visible to the naked eye.

Fecal samples can also be examined under the microscope to demonstrate the presence of intestinal parasites. By performing an autopsy on a fish that has just died, the veterinarian can evaluate the internal organs and note any changes that would point to specific diseases.

If the skin of your fish is affected, the veterinarian can also run a bacteriological test. This will reveal which pathogens are involved and which antibiotics are appropriate for controlling them. Most bacteria that infect fish are resistant to a great many antibiotics and, consequently, can be controlled successfully only with special antibiotics that have proven to be effective.

265. Discontinuing Medications: What must I keep in mind once I have finished treating my fish with a medication?

Once treatment with a medication is finished, you should carry out a partial water change. In order to get rid of any residual medication, you should add activated carbon to the filter or put a small internal filter with activated carbon in the tank. Be sure to remove the activated carbon again after two to three days. Otherwise the drug residues that it has filtered out could eventually get back into the aquarium.

Do not forget to disinfect all the equipment, such as nets or algae magnets. Pathogens could adhere to them and trigger a new outbreak of the infection.

266. Disease Prevention: Are there ways to prevent my aquarium fish from getting sick?

The answer is a definite yes. Pay close attention to the following preventive measures.

➤ Quarantine tank: The easiest way to prevent the introduction of disease is by holding all new arrivals in a quarantine tank for at least 14 days.

➤ Water: The proper water quality is important. That is why you should test the water parameters in your tank regularly. Consistently good water quality is an important prerequisite for the well-being of your fish.

➤ Stocking level: The stocking level in the aquarium should not be too high. The more fish you have in your tank, the greater the stress and risk of infection.

➤ Feeding: You must give your fish a varied diet. This ensures that they are getting all their necessary vitamins and other nutrients, and it prevents the occurrence of nutritional deficiencies.

Important: Many diseases, especially bacterial infections, are so-called multifactorial diseases. This means that the bacteria will make your fish sick only if conditions in the tank are not optimal.

This is one reason why it is important to keep a close watch on water conditions in the tank. You may be able to prevent the outbreak of sickness among your fish.

267. Disease Susceptibility: Is it true that fish are robust creatures?

Unfortunately, this is not always the case. Fish are very sensitive to environmental influences. In addition, there are more than a thousand species of parasites that can attack fish.

In the wild, almost all fish are troubled to some extent by parasites. With good environmental conditions and a strong immune system, they can normally cope well. If the fish are kept in an aquarium, however, various stress factors can quickly trigger disease—for example, too little room or too many fish, resulting in an increased risk of infection. If the fish's immune system is not in top shape, then parasites and bacteria have an easy game.

Many an aquarist has had to learn about fish diseases the hard way. That is why you should quarantine new arrivals, make sure conditions in your tank are appropriate for the species living there, and give your fish the right food. If you do this, then you will have laid the groundwork for the good health of your aquarium fish. Keep in mind that a single diseased fish let loose in your aquarium can wreak havoc among all of the tank's residents.

EXTRA TIP

UV Sterilizer
If your fish are susceptible to disease, you can use a UV clarifier/sterilizer to minimize the risk of infection. In this device, the tank water is pumped past a UV lamp. The ultraviolet rays kill off disease-causing bacteria along with some algae and unicellular organisms. Caution—Do not use a UV lamp when you are medicating the tank. Many medications are broken down under UV light and lose their effectiveness.

268. Euthanasia: What do I do with my seriously ill fish? Should I put it out of its misery? How can I do that so the fish does not suffer?

If a fish is incurably ill, it should be killed painlessly. Leaving a terminally ill fish to suffer is not humane behavior. You would not let a family dog or cat suffer, so you should not let your fish suffer.

You will frequently see freezing suggested as a humane method to kill fish, but this is not advisable. Although fish fall into a sort of torpor due to low temperature, they do not lose consciousness.

Sometimes a dying fish is flushed down the toilet, but this is extremely cruel. The fish is shocked by the radical change in water quality and then dies slowly and painfully in the sewers.

A humane method is to sever the spine behind the head with a pair of scissors. Most fish owners have a hard time bringing themselves to do this, though.

In this case, the pet shop can euthanize the fish. The sick fish is placed into a small tank and the pet shop owner adds an overdose of anesthetic directly to the water.

EXTRA TIP

Euthanasia with clove oil
Eugenol, the active ingredient in clove oil, anesthetizes fish. After prolonged exposure, the fish will not wake up again. Place the fish into a bucket with 1–2 quarts (1–2 L) of water. Add about 5 drops of clove oil per quart (liter). Once the fish goes to sleep, increase the dose to about 20 drops per quart (liter). Since the concentration of eugenol in clove oil varies, higher amounts may be necessary. Once the gills have been motionless for a while and there is no eye reflex, the fish is dead.

269. Eye Diseases: One of my Guppies has something wrong with one eye. Could it have an eye disease?

Eye diseases are not uncommon in fish. If your fish was injured, a distinct change in the eye could persist after the wound healed. Infections due to bacteria or parasites can also cause eye diseases. The condition called pop eye can develop in gas bubble disease, but it can also be due to general infections like fish tuberculosis. Changes in the eyes are usually indications of a serious disease. I recommend you consult a veterinarian or your pet shop if you believe that your fish have contracted an eye disease.

270. Eyes Protruding: All of a sudden, the eyes of some of my aquarium fish are bulging. What is causing that?

One of the most common causes of the condition known as pop eye, or exophthalmus, is an infection with mycobacteria, the pathogen that causes fish tuberculosis.

In this disease, ulcers and nodules (granulomas) develop in the internal organs and sometimes in the skin as well as in the eye sockets. This forces the eyeballs to protrude.

Unfortunately, this disease is incurable; furthermore, the bacteria may be able to infect humans and cause a skin disease. On the other hand, your fish could be suffering from gas bubble disease.

A veterinarian who specializes in fish can diagnose or possibly rule out tuberculosis by examining a sick fish. To avoid a potentially serious health problem in your aquarium, you should consult a veterinarian if you notice that one of your fish has protruding eyes.

271. Filter Bacteria and Medications: At present, I am treating my sick fish with a medication that I add directly to the water. Should I remove the filter so that the filter bacteria are not harmed?

No, let the filter continue to run, even if the filter bacteria could be harmed by some medications, such as antibiotics. It is true that you will often see the advice to disconnect the filter when medicating the tank to avoid harming the filter bacteria. However, the disease-causing organisms are in the filter, too, and they will stay there after it is disconnected. When the treatment is over, these pathogens will get back into the aquarium through the filter and could trigger another infection.

To avoid contaminating the water with nitrogenous wastes resulting from uneaten food, give the fish little or nothing to eat during the treatment. Sick fish usually lose their appetite, anyway.

272. Fish Lice: Are there really lice that can infest fish?

Yes, fish lice—which include carp lice—do indeed exist. Zoologically speaking, fish lice are crustaceans, not actual lice.

They primarily attack Goldfish and Koi as well as other small fish kept in ponds. Occasionally, carp lice (*Argulus* sp.) are found in aquarium fish, too.

The parasites are usually introduced with live foods. Measuring about $1/4$ inch (5–7 mm) in length, they are visible to the naked eye. They suck the blood out of the infected fish through a spine; this can even be fatal in small specimens like Neon Tetras. These parasites do not just harm their hosts by sucking blood, though. They can also transmit pathogens like bacteria and viruses. If only a few fish are infested with carp lice, then you can remove the parasites with a blunt pair of tweezers or give the fish a salt bath.

273. **Fish Tuberculosis: What is fish tuberculosis, and how do I recognize this disease?**

Fish tuberculosis, also called mycobacteriosis, is caused by mycobacteria belonging to the same genus as the bacteria that cause tuberculosis in humans and mammals. These pathogens affect not just fish but other cold-blooded animals like amphibians and reptiles as well. In fish, the bacteria cause nodules (granulomas) in the internal organs, especially the spleen and kidneys. The organs become enlarged as a result, and the fish's abdomen swells. In this disease, ulcers frequently develop on the skin and around the eyes. If a granuloma forms behind the eyeball, this can lead to the condition called pop eye. Sometimes the affected fish develop curvature of the spine. There are not always externally visible signs, though. Some fish just stop eating, lose weight, and die.

EXTRA TIP

Removing carp lice
If you want to remove individual carp lice, take the fish out of the tank with a net. While, leaving the fish in the net, hold it gently in a towel so that you can pluck off the parasites with a fine pair of tweezers. If the carp lice are very numerous or if all the fish are infested, then the veterinarian or pet shop can recommend a medication to control them.

274. Fish Tuberculosis: **What causes an outbreak of fish tuberculosis, and how can a diseased fish be treated?**

Fish tuberculosis is a multifactorial disease. This means that after an infection with mycobacteria, the disease appears only if the living conditions are poor. Prevention is thus the best way to protect your fish. Provide optimal environmental conditions, and be conscientious about quarantining new arrivals.

Fish tuberculosis is incurable, even though there are references in the literature to supposedly successful treatments with specific antibiotics.

Mycobacteria can be identified in the organs of infected fish using a specific dye. Tests like this are carried out in a laboratory or by the veterinarian.

If the fish in a tank have been diagnosed with fish tuberculosis, I suggest the following.

➤ If the disease is chronic, which means that now and then a fish dies exhibiting the typical symptoms, you can continue to keep the outwardly healthy fish. However, do not add any new fish.

On the one hand, new arrivals will mean stress for the resident fish, which favors an outbreak of the disease. On the other hand, the new fish can be infected themselves and die.

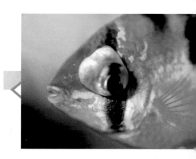

Signs of fish tuberculosis vary depending on the infection. Sometimes the eyes are affected (pop eye).

➤ If all the fish are affected, they should be euthanized. Then you have to clean and disinfect the tank and all the equipment thoroughly (preferably with a tuberculocidal product from the drugstore) before you can set it up again and stock it with new fish.

As a general rule, be careful when working in the aquarium! Be sure to wear rubber gloves, because fish tuberculosis can be transmitted to humans.

If you have open sores on your hands and your immune system is weakened, these bacteria can penetrate the skin and produce lesions (so-called swimming pool granuloma). These skin lesions usually clear up on their own after a few weeks to months. If necessary, consult a physician.

275. Frayed Fins: My Guppies have frayed fins. Why is that, and what can I do about it?

Your Guppies are suffering from fin rot. This disease is caused by a bacterial infection that leads to inflammations that erode the affected parts of the fins. The bacteria become a problem especially if the water quality is poor, which weakens the immune system of the fish. Unicellular parasites are often involved in the disease process as well. They injure the fish's skin and create a portal of entry for the bacteria.

The disease can be cured by antibiotics. In addition, you have to provide optimal water quality that satisfies the requirements of your fish and take the appropriate measures to remove any parasites present. When given the proper treatment, the fins of your Guppies will usually grow back completely.

If the prescribed treatment does not seem to be working consult your veterinarian. He or she should be able to take care of the problem.

276. Grayish Coating on the Skin: Our fish have a velvety gray coating on the skin. What is that?

Usually coatings like this are caused by unicellular skin parasites like *Oodinium* or *Costia*. The fish then frequently scrape themselves against rocks, driftwood, or plants.

The disease caused by *Oodinium* is also known as velvet disease since a velvety gray coating develops on the skin of the fish.

These pear-shaped or spherical flagellates infect the skin and gills and feed on the tissue fluids of the fish. Heavier infestations can lead to inflammatory skin reactions or even extensive peeling away of the skin. If the gills are affected, difficulty in breathing results.

Costia, a bean-shaped flagellate, also attacks the skin and gills. In addition to a gray filmy coating, lesions that extend into the musculature can appear in advanced stages. This parasite is referred to as a debility parasite because, in addition to infecting young fish, it primarily attacks fish with weakened immune systems.

The veterinarian can determine which pathogens are actually at work here by examining a skin smear under the microscope.

If necessary, these parasites can be treated with medications containing malachite green or copper, available from the pet store.

Sometimes, though, bacterial infections are responsible for this condition, in which case they must be treated with antibiotics.

In any case, you should check the water parameters, since bad water quality can also cause pathological changes in the skin. You should rule out poor water quality as a possible cause of grayish skin before you consult your veterinarian.

277. Loss of Appetite: My fish have stopped eating and are very apathetic. What could be causing this?

Making a definite diagnosis based on these two disease signs is not easy. First check to make sure the water parameters are in order. One possible cause for loss of appetite and changes in behavior could be an infestation with worms. An affected fish can display a variety of symptoms. It seems apathetic, its skin turns dark, it loses weight despite eating well, or it refuses to eat. The best thing to do is take your fish to a veterinarian or your pet shop.

278. Medications from the Veterinarian: The pet store sells medications for a wide range of fish diseases. Are there also drugs that I can obtain only from a veterinarian?

There are a few, but in the United States most therapeutic agents used to treat aquarium fish can be obtained without a prescription. These include antibiotics and preparations used to control parasites. You can get nonprescription medications from the pet store. Pay careful attention to the instructions in the package insert. You should also ask the veterinarian or an expert aquarist for advice on the dosage and administration of any medication.

279. Neon Tetra Disease: What is neon tetra disease? How are fish infected with it?

Neon tetra disease affects Neon Tetras in particular—hence the name—as well as other characins and, very rarely, barbs or cichlids. It is caused by unicellular parasites called sporozoans that embed themselves in the musculature of the fish and destroy it.

The fish are infected by ingesting the parasite along with their food. External features of this disease are relatively easy to recognize. The colors of the fish fade, especially on the body, and there is a noticeable decrease of their schooling behavior. Unfortunately, neon tetra disease is incurable. Affected fish should be euthanized.

280. Parasites: What criteria can be used to distinguish the different types of parasites?

On the one hand, parasites can be divided into those that occur externally (ectoparasites) and those found inside the body (endoparasites). They can also be divided into unicellular and multicellular parasites. Unicellular parasites are always so small that they can be seen only under the microscope, while multi-cellular parasites can often be seen with the naked eye.

Ectoparasites attach themselves to the skin and gills of fish. They include multicellular skin and gill flukes, fish leeches, and numerous unicellular parasites, e.g., *Ichthyophthirius*, *Costia*, and *Trichodina*.

EXTRA TIP

Visible parasites
Fish leeches grow to 1¼ inches (3 cm) in length and primarily affect Koi and Goldfish. Anchor worms (*Lernea*), which get up to 1½ inches (4 cm) long, prefer to attack the skin of Goldfish. Gill copepods (family Ergasilidae) are visible as elongated, white dots on the gills of fish when you lift the gill cover. *Camallanus* worms are parasitic nematodes that live in the lower intestine of live-bearing toothcarps, characins, barbs, and cichlids.

Among the endoparasites are tapeworms and nematodes as well as unicellular parasites like hexamitids or coccidians that primarily infect the intestine.

Parasites must be treated with special medications depending on the species.

281. Pathogens: I have three aquariums. An infectious disease has broken out in one of them. How can I prevent the pathogens from being spread from one tank to another?

?

You can prevent the spread of disease-causing organisms from one tank to another by having individual, specially marked equipment for each tank and using it exclusively for the designated tank. If you do not do this, you must be conscientious about carefully cleaning all equipment, such as algae magnets or nets, after each use and then disinfecting them, for example in a pan containing 5 percent formalin (from the drug store). Caution: Put the pan into a well-ventilated area and do not inhale the fumes!

You should always take care of the tank with the sick fish last. You should also be very careful not to transfer a spray bar, decorations, or plants from the infected tank into another aquarium. After you have finished all of the maintenance chores in the tank

EXTRA TIP

Short-term bath before treating the entire tank
First give one or two sick fish a short-term bath. To do this, fill a small spare tank with aquarium water from the existing tank, add the proper dose of medication, and then put in the fish. Watch their behavior closely for at least 24 hours. If they show no signs of intolerance, you can treat the main tank.

with the sick fish, be sure to wash your hands carefully and disinfect them. You can get suitable disinfectants for you hands at the drugstore.

282. Poisoning: Can fish be poisoned in an aquarium? How can I tell if a fish has been poisoned?

Poisoning is not uncommon in aquarium fish. It is often manifested by general changes in behavior. The fish are uncoordinated when they swim, hang at the water surface, shoot wildly through the water, have difficulty breathing, are apathetic, are easily startled, look pale, or appear brightly colored. The clinical features of poisoning are quite diverse.

If you suspect poisoning, then you should immediately check the water.

➤ Copper poisoning can be caused by things like new copper pipes or a continuous-flow water heater. Catfish, such as bristlenose catfish (*Ancistrus* spp.) or dwarf suckermouth catfish (*Otocinclus* spp.), are particularly sensitive to copper. However, copper in the aquarium water usually comes from algae control products or from medications that the aquarist has added to the tank.

➤ Water from old lead pipes can cause lead poisoning.

➤ Be careful when using insecticides around the aquarium. For example, if you are treating your houseplants for aphids or your dog for fleas, never do it in the room where your aquarium is located. Most insecticides are highly toxic to fish.

➤ If you use paints, varnishes, and solvents in the same room as the aquarium, the fumes can poison your fish.

If the problem persists, you should consult your veterinarian. He or she should be able to diagnose the problem and offer a solution.

283. Salt Bath: Why is it often recommended to add salt to the water for sick fish?

Salt is one of the oldest fish medications. If you add common salt to the water in your aquarium, it increases the resistance of the fish. When stimulated by the salt, the fish produce more slime on their body surface. This helps repel harmful bacteria and parasites and thus reduces their number. In addition, salt inhibits the reproduction of bacteria in the water.

➤ Concentrated salt bath in a spare tank: In order to treat external parasites like fish leeches, set up a spare tank with aquarium water. Then put the affected fish into the tank and gradually add salt to the water (up to 2 ounces of salt per gallon of water/15 g/l).

However, the fish should stay in water with this much salt for only a short time, 20 minutes at most. Be sure to watch the fish very carefully during the salt bath. If you notice any sign of intolerance, end the bath at once and immediately return the fish to the original tank.

284. Scraping: Why do my fish scrape themselves against the aquarium decorations?

When fish scrape themselves against rocks, driftwood, plants, or the substrate, this indicates that their skin and/or gills are irritated. The cause could be unicellular or multicellular parasites, such as *Trichodina,* or skin and gill flukes. Often the only thing pointing to an infestation with *Trichodina* is the behavior of the fish (scraping), because nothing can be seen on the skin itself. This circular ciliate anchors itself in the skin and gills. It is often found together with skin

flukes (family Gyro-
dactylidae). These are
trematodes that use
their hold-fast organ,
the haptor, to anchor
themselves in the skin
of the fish and feed on
its skin cells. They
often trigger a bacterial
infection that can lead
to deep-seated damage
to the skin. Gill flukes
(family Dactylogyri-
dae) are also trema-
todes and attach
themselves to the gills
with their hold-fast
organ. Signs of infec-
tion include scraping
the gill region against
objects, jerky move-

> **INFO**
>
> **Introducing
> parasites**
> Parasites can get into the
> aquarium in a variety of
> ways. For one thing, they
> can be brought in by new
> fish that are put in with
> the existing fish without
> first being quarantined.
> They can also be intro-
> duced through live foods,
> new plants that come from
> an infected aquarium, or
> tank accessories that have
> not been disinfected.

ments of the head, darting through the water, gasping
for air at the water surface, and rapid breathing.
These parasites can be controlled with formalin baths
or medications. Your veterinarian or pet shop can
advise you about treatments. You should also test the
water parameters and correct them if necessary. If the
pH is too acidic or alkaline, this can also be responsible for the fish scraping themselves.

285. Signs of Disease: **How can I tell if a fish
is sick?**

You can recognize a sick fish by the following signs:
➤ It appears emaciated and its head is large in proportion to its body. In the terminal stage, the fish
often has a so-called knife back.

➤ The fish stops eating.
➤ The fish's abdomen is bloated (swollen belly).
➤ The fish changes its swimming or social behavior. Here are a few examples. The fish seems apathetic, wobbles when it swims, stays in the corner, hides, shoots through the water, scrapes against the aquarium wall or decorations, the flight reflex is not triggered when you approach the fish with a net or your hand, schooling fish keep to themselves, species that are normally in constant motion now stay on the bottom.
➤ The fish changes color or becomes pale and transparent.
➤ The body surface changes. The skin has discolored areas, growths, coatings, or ulcers. Bloody spots or patches are visible.
➤ The scales stand out from the body, giving it a pinecone-like appearance.
➤ The fins are frayed or entirely absent except for a few fin rays.
➤ The fish do not use their fins when moving but, instead, hold them close to the body (called fin clamping).
➤ One or both eyes are abnormal, may seem to protrude (called pop eye), or appear enlarged.
➤ The spine is curved.
➤ Breathing is abnormal. The fish hangs at the surface of the water, and the gill covers are flared or move faster than usual when the fish breathes. The gills appear swollen and/or do not have the normal red color.
➤ The feces are abnormal. Only slimy white feces are produced.

If you think that your fish have contracted a disease, you should consult your veterinarian. The sooner you treat the problem, the more likely your fish will return to good health.

DISEASES OF ENVIRONMENTAL ORIGIN

DISEASE	SYMPTOM / POSSIBLE CAUSE / NEXT STEP
Oxygen deficiency	➤ Fish hang at the water surface and gasp for air, die with mouth wide open ➤ Insufficient oxygen due to decaying organic matter, too many plants, and no aeration ➤ Improved aeration, partial water change
Ammonia poisoning	➤ Central nervous system disorders, loss of appetite, rapid death ➤ Too much ammonia in the water due to organic wastes, alkaline pH ➤ Partial water change
Acidosis or alkalosis	➤ Increased slime production by the skin, fish shoot through the water, labored breathing ➤ pH too high or too low ➤ Partial water change, add buffers (calcium carbonate) if pH is too acidic
Problems caused by improper temperature	➤ Temperature too low: Apathy, loss of appetite, fin clamping ➤ Temperature too high: Increased activity at first, then apathy, labored breathing ➤ Raise temperature with a water heater or lower it with cold water
Obesity (adipositas)	➤ Rounded body shape, distended belly ➤ Overfeeding ➤ Feed less
Vitamin deficiency	➤ Various, some nonspecific ➤ Dry food is too old or improperly stored ➤ Store dry food in a cool, dry place; use it within three months of opening the container
Egg binding	➤ Distended belly in females ➤ Insufficient opportunity to spawn, no males present ➤ Provide places to spawn, e.g., fine-leaved plants; keep males and females in the same tank

286. Skin with Black Spots: Two of my fish have little black spots all over their body. Could this be a dangerous disease?

If these black spots are not part of the natural coloration of your fish, it could be black spot disease. This is caused by an infestation with larval flukes (trematodes) that lodge in the skin. They appear as elongated black nodules a fraction of an inch (several mm) long.

Flukes need various intermediate hosts for their development, such as snails, fish, and birds. Therefore the disease occurs in only wild-caught fish. In the aquarium, the developmental cycle cannot be completed because the intermediate hosts are missing. Thus the disease is limited to just a few animals and cannot be transmitted to other fish. The larvae usually fall off by themselves after a while and die, so you do not need to do anything for a mild infestation that does not harm the fish. However, if the fish are severely affected, treatment with a suitable medication will help.

287. Skin with Holes: My discus have small holes in the skin of their head. What could that be?

Your fish are suffering from what is known as hole-in-the-head disease. It can be triggered by deficiencies in calcium and vitamin D, which arise especially when discus are fed beef heart or an unbalanced

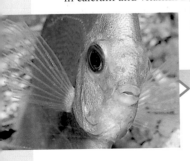

Hole-in-the-head disease in discus can frequently be ascribed to vitamin and mineral deficiencies.

beef heart mixture. Switching to a good brand-name food and/or supplementing the food with preparations containing vitamin D and calcium can help. Another possible cause for hole-in-the-head disease is an infection of the intestine with unicellular flagellates known as hexamitids. To make a diagnosis, the veterinarian should examine a fecal sample for parasites under the microscope. If there is a hexamitid infestation, the veterinarian can prescribe a suitable medication to treat it.

288. Skin with White Spots: My Goldfish have small white spots on their body. What are they?

Male goldfish can develop so-called breeding tubercles during the spawning period in spring. These are visible as small, whitish spots on the head. This is not a sign of disease; the fish are lively and behave normally.

However, if the fish have tiny white spots scattered over the entire body and they show signs of illness such as rubbing themselves against decorations, fin clamping, or loss of appetite, then they probably have white spot disease. This is caused by a unicellular parasitic ciliate, *Ichthyophthirius multifiliis*, which is why aquarists refer to the disease as ich. A variety of medications effective against these single-celled organisms are available at the pet store.

If, during the spring and summer, you keep your goldfish in a garden pond where mussels also live, then there is another possible cause for this symptom. Mussel larvae, called glochidia, can implant themselves in the skin of the fish, where they appear as whitish dots. The mussel larvae leave the fish of their own accord after a few weeks. You do not have to add any medications to the water, especially since the fish are normally not bothered very much. These mussels, which are more likely to be kept in garden ponds than in aquariums, are even useful because they filter the water.

289. Snails: **The snails in my aquarium are all hanging at the surface of the water. What does that mean?** ·

If your snails are behaving abnormally, then you should immediately check the water parameters, particularly oxygen, nitrate, nitrite, and ammonia levels and pH. Snails can be much more sensitive to environmental disturbances or chemical substances than fish. Snails—assuming they are gill-breathing species—usually show abnormal behavior sooner than fish if the water is polluted or the oxygen level is too low.

290. Snails Dying: **The snails in my aquarium are dying. What could be causing this?**

If your snails are dying, this can be for a number of reasons. Various infections caused by bacteria, viruses, or parasites can kill snails.

It is also possible that the water quality is not optimal for the snails. They are more sensitive to certain substances than fish.

In addition, many medications and algae control products are toxic to snails. Many snail species, for instance the Apple Snail (*Ampullaria gigas*), cannot tolerate very soft water for any length of time because it does not contain enough calcium, which is important for their shell. Consequently, the snail shells become porous and, before long, the snails die.

291. Spawning: **One of my female Tiger Barbs has a distended abdomen. I suspect that she is pregnant, but she is not spawning. What could be the reason for this?**

A swollen abdomen can be caused by a variety of factors. The female could be egg bound. This can happen if she has no opportunity to spawn. Provide your female with a suitable spot to lay her eggs. You could, for example, put fine-leaved plants into the tank. You should also keep females and males together in the same tank. This way the male will stimulate the female to spawn.

292. Swollen Abdomen: **One of my fish has a swollen abdomen. What could cause that?**

A swollen abdomen can develop if the fish is constantly overfed and gains weight as a result. This may also be a female full of eggs. If a pregnant female has a swollen belly and has not spawned, she is probably egg bound.

Some species of fish like Balloon Mollies have an extremely shortened spine that makes them appear bloated. In many Goldfish varieties, an enlarged abdomen is even part of the breed standard and is thus a result of selective breeding. However, a swollen belly can also be a sign of a serious disease like organ tumors or fish tuberculosis. If it is the latter, then often the eyes will protrude as well and/or ulcers will be visible on the surface of the body. In Goldfish, a parasite (*Hoferellus carassii*) can attack the kidneys, which then respond by becoming massively enlarged. In the terminal stage, the affected fish appears monstrously bloated. If there are signs of disease, you should immediately consult a veterinarian or your pet shop.

293. Transporting Fish: What is the best way to transport my fish to the pet shop?

I recommend you use plastic bags with rounded corners, available at the pet store, to transport your fish to the pet shop. Fill the bag halfway with aquarium water, leaving the remainder filled with air. Put the fish into the water, and close the bag tightly with a rubber band. Wrap the bag in an insulating layer of newspaper to maintain the water temperature. If the pet shop is not too far away, you can also use a bucket with a lid to transport the fish.

For small fish like Neon Tetras or Guppies, you should take along three or four sick individuals. Being able to observe and examine several animals makes it easier to make a diagnosis.

If you would like to bring a dead fish for examination, I suggest you keep it chilled. The easiest way to keep the fish cold is to surround it with freezer packs. Chilling is especially important in warm weather.

294. Unusual Behavior: My fish are swimming at the water surface, hanging around the filter outlet, and gasping for air. Why are they doing that?

Your fish are suffering from hypoxia, a lack of oxygen. One reason could be that the aquarium water contains too little dissolved oxygen. Your fish are trying to take advantage of the water entering the aquarium from the filter, which is somewhat better oxygenated. In any case, measure the oxygen level of the water right away (using a test kit from the pet store). If it is too low (less than 4 ppm), you should immediately carry out a partial water change. You can also improve the aeration by installing a diaphragm air pump with an airstone. Check the water temperature, too, because the oxygen level drops as temperature rises. If necessary, turn down the heater.

Another reason your fish might not be getting enough oxygen is that their gills may have been damaged, perhaps by a heavy infestation with parasites or a bacterial infection. This would prevent oxygen from being absorbed properly through the gills. In this case, too, you can take the steps described above. You still have to use medications to control the parasites or the infection, though. The pet shop can advise you here.

295. Unusual Behavior: My fish are breathing rapidly, shooting through the water, and even trying to jump out of the tank. What does that mean?

This behavior suggests acidosis or alkalosis. It occurs when the pH of the aquarium water is very acidic (below 5) or very alkaline (over 8.5). This burns the gills and skin of the fish so that they react as you describe.

Check the water, especially the pH. To remedy the situation, immediately change about half the aquarium water, and then after a few hours, carry out another partial water change. Never transfer the fish to another tank in which the water has the desired pH or even a neutral pH. The fish will not tolerate this sudden change and may even die right away.

In general, if your fish appear to be displaying abnormal behavior, you should check the tank's water parameters immediately. If you have ruled out water as a cause of unusual behavior, you check the fish themselves.

296. Unusual Behavior: Lately my fish have been darting back and forth though the tank. What can that mean?

If all the fish in the aquarium are behaving this way, it is probably due to poisoning. Poisoning often occurs as a result of mistakes in husbandry, for instance elevated levels of nitrite or ammonia due to inactive filter bacteria, use of the wrong medication, or medication overdoses. Tap water that runs through copper pipes (common in older buildings) or heavily chlorinated water can also lead to severe poisoning. As first aid, I recommend you carry out a partial water change. You can remove chlorine by aerating the water vigorously in a bucket or by simply letting it stand for two days before adding it to the tank.

297. Using Medications: What general rules must I follow when treating my fish with medications?

Observe your fish especially carefully during the treatment. If you notice that they are not tolerating the medication, then you must stop treatment immediately and change the water or else move the fish.

INFO

Administering medications

Medications for ornamental fish are usually added directly to the water, and the fish absorb the active ingredients through their gills and skin. Although commercial fisheries usually give medications in food, this method of administration is rarely used for ornamental fish. With larger fish like Koi, the veterinarian can even inject the medication with a hypodermic syringe.

If you move the fish, you need a second tank that you can set up like a quarantine tank.

Signs of possible drug intolerance include the fish shimmying, lying on their side, darting through the tank, being extremely apathetic, or breathing very rapidly.

I recommend you observe the following guidelines when using medications.

➤ Administer medications only to treat a disease, never as a prophylactic (preventive) measure.

➤ Have the veterinarian make a precise diagnosis of the disease so that your fish can get the right medication.

➤ Ask the veterinarian or pet shop if the selected medication will be tolerated by all occupants of the aquarium (including snails, freshwater shrimp, and so on).

➤ Use the medication at the proper dosage; it can be ineffective at too low a dose and harmful if the dose is too high.

➤ Never put two medications into the aquarium water at the same time unless the veterinarian has instructed you to do so. Otherwise there can be adverse interactions.

➤ Water conditioners should never be added to the tank along with medications, because many water conditioners contain complexing agents that will bind medications and render them ineffective.

➤ Let the filter continue to run during the treatment. Do not add activated carbon to the filter, because this absorbs the medications and destroys their effectiveness.

➤ Switch off the UV sterilizer since medications are quickly broken down under UV light and cannot achieve their full effect.

➤ Once the treatment is finished, you should remove the medication from the water using activated carbon and change 20–30 percent of the water several days in a row.

298. Veterinarian: Should I consult the veterinarian right away when one or more of my fish is sick?

First make sure the individual water parameters are in order and meet the requirements of your fish. If the values are within acceptable limits, I urge you to consult a veterinarian who specializes in fish. You can get addresses from your state or local veterinary medical society or from address listings on the Internet.

The veterinarian can usually diagnose a disease quickly and prescribe the proper treatment. I advise against haphazardly trying a variety of different medications.

299. Veterinarian's fees: What should I expect to pay when I have a veterinarian examine my sick fish?

Giving a general answer is impossible since the fees depend on the type and extent of the examination as well as the time involved. You should discuss this beforehand with your veterinarian. He or she can certainly give you an estimate after you have described the problem.

300. Viral diseases: Do fish get viral diseases? If so, how can they be treated?

Fish can indeed be infected by a virus. Viruses are much smaller than bacteria and replicate in the cells of the host. Lymphocystis is an example of a viral disease. Here the virus induces cauliflower-like growths of the skin cells. This disease occurs particularly often in larger labyrinth fish. Carp pox is also caused by a virus. Unfortunately, viral diseases cannot be treated with medications. They either kill the fish, or else the fish's immune system manages to overcome the infection on its own. Have a sick fish examined and evaluated by a pet shop that specializes in fish.

301. White Feces: My Angelfish are producing white feces. What does that mean?

There could be several reasons why your fish are eliminating white feces.

➤ Perhaps your fish have had little or nothing to eat. The white, stringy feces would then consist of sloughed off intestinal cells (they renew themselves every 24 hours). Observe the feeding behavior of your Angelfish carefully. If there is no change, you should go to the veterinarian.

➤ Hexamitids in the intestine could also be responsible for the whitish feces. These are unicellular parasites that attack the intestine, where they provoke an inflammation. In this case, the problem can be treated with metronidazole, a nonprescription drug.

➤ Sometimes white feces can also indicate an infestation with worms. Your veterinarian can determine whether there are worms in your fish's intestines by examining a fecal sample and then, if necessary, initiate the appropriate treatment.

302. Worms: Can fish actually be infested with worms? How can I tell if a fish has worms?

Fish, like other vertebrates, can play host to different types of worms.

➤ Skin flukes and gill flukes are visible only under the microscope. If fish are infested with skin flukes, they often scrape themselves against rocks or plants and make repeated vigorous swallowing movements. These flukes frequently damage the skin, which can then become infected by bacteria. Gill flukes live in the gills of fish, where they cause inflammations of the tissues. In heavy infestations, the fish have difficulty breathing.

➤ Various types of nematodes and tapeworms are found in the intestinal tract. Fish that are infected by these worms often appear emaciated.

➤ Many other types of worms or their larvae can attack almost every organ in the fish and cause a wide range of symptoms. The affected animal may appear apathetic, its skin may turn dark, or it may lose its appetite. The best thing you can do is consult your pet shop.

The pet shop will be able to determine which worms are involved and prescribe the appropriate treatment. Unfortunately, there is no universal anti-worm drug.

303. **Worms: My Angelfish have tiny red worms or parts of worms hanging out of the anus. What are they, and how can I get rid of them?**

Your Angelfish are probably infested with parasitic intestinal nematodes (*Camallanus* sp.). These worms inhabit the lower section of the intestine, particularly in live-bearing toothcarps, characins, barbs, and cichlids. You can sometimes see the tail end of the worm sticking out of the fish's anus.

Incidentally, the red color is due to the fish's blood on which they feed.

These parasites can be very stubborn. The best remedy is a prescription medication from the veterinarian that is also used to control parasitic worms in other animals.

Once you notice that your fish have been infested with worms, you should seek medical care. The sooner you treat the problem, the better off your fish will be.

304. Worms: **Little worms are swimming around in my aquarium. Are they harmful for my fish?**

These free-swimming creatures are probably aquatic oligochaete worms known as naidids. They eat dead and rotting plant matter or fish food that has sunk to the bottom of the aquarium; they will not harm your fish. Naidids often disappear on their own.

Feed your fish as little as possible. That will reduce the worms' food supply and curb their reproduction. If these worms bother you, you can also get rid of them with a medication from your pet shop.

305. Zoonoses: **Are there diseases that can be transmitted from fish to humans?**

There are indeed diseases that can be transmitted from fish to humans; they are called zoonoses. One of these is fish tuberculosis. This bacterial infection can be triggered by coming in contact with infected fish or working in infected aquarium water. In humans, the pathogen enters through small open wounds and causes skin lesions. If you suspect your fish have fish tuberculosis or if you have unhealed cuts on your hands, you can protect yourself from infection by wearing rubber gloves whenever you work in the aquarium.

There are also other pathogenic bacteria, for example salmonella, that can infect humans.

Angelfish (Pterophyllum scalare) *as well as other fish can be attacked by* Camallanus *worms.*

306. Zoonoses: **Which precautions should I take so that I am not infected by fish diseases that can be transmitted to humans?**

If you have open wounds on your hands, you should wear rubber gloves when you work in the aquarium. When you are using a siphon hose to change the water, never suck on the hose to start the water flowing. If you do, you could accidentally swallow infected aquarium water.

Instead, always work with a principle of physics—the siphon. Fill the hose with water at the faucet or in a sink and close the ends with your thumbs, making sure no air remains in the hose. Hold one end of the hose in the aquarium water, place the other into a bucket on the floor below the tank. First open the end of the hose that is in the aquarium and then

When working in the aquarium, always pay attention to good hygiene.

the end in the bucket. The water will begin to flow immediately. To stop the flow of water, simply use your thumb to close the end of the hose in the bucket.

Pet stores also sell hoses equipped with a special siphon starter.

Index

Appendix

Addresses

Clubs/Associations

American Cichlid Association
www.cichlid.org

American Killifish Association
www.aka.org

American Livebearer Association
http://livebearers.org

Federation of American Aquarium Societies (provides links to local aquarium clubs)
www.faas.info

Goldfish Society of America
www.goldfishsociety.org

International Betta Congress
www.ibcbettas.com

International Fancy Guppy Association
www.ifga.org

International Rainbowfish Association
www.irg-online.de

North American Native Fishes Association
www.nanfa.org

Fish-Keeping on the Internet

FINS: The Fish Information Service (articles, links, and directories on fishkeeping)
http://fins.actwin.com

FishBase (an excellent searchable database providing exhaustive information on over 29,700 species of fish)
www.fishbase.org

FishIndex (a searchable database of freshwater and saltwater aquarium fish, invertebrates, and plants; includes species profiles, forums, and conversion calculators)
www.fishindex.com

FishLinkCentral (aquarium resources on the Internet)
www.fishlinkcentral.com

PetEducation (articles on pet healthcare from Drs. Foster and Smith)
www.peteducation.com

Planet Catfish (an excellent source of information on catfish)
www.planetcatfish.com

Pet Sitters

National Association of Professional Pet Sitters
800-296-PETS
www.petsitters.org

Pet Sitters International
336-983-9222
www.petsit.com

Books

Blasiola, George. *Koi*. Barron's Educational Series, Inc., Hauppauge, NY, 2005.

Elson, Gary, and Oliver Lucanus. *Catfish.* Barron's Educational Series, Inc., Hauppauge, NY, 2003.

Fairfield, Terry. *A Commonsense Guide to Fish Health.* Barron's Educational Series, Inc., Hauppauge, NY, 2000.

Giovanetti, Thomas, and Oliver Lucanus. *Discus Fish.* Barron's Educational Series, Inc., Hauppauge, NY, 2005.

Goldstein, Robert J. *Angelfish.* Barron's Educational Series, Inc., Hauppauge, NY, 2001.

———. *The Betta Handbook.* Barron's Educational Series, Inc., Hauppauge, NY, 2004.

Gula, Wolfgang. *Plants for Your Aquarium.* Barron's Educational Series, Inc., Hauppauge, NY, 2002.

Hiscock, Peter. *Aquarium Designs Inspired by Nature.* Barron's Educational Series, Inc., Hauppauge, NY, 2003.

———. *Aquarium Plants.* Barron's Educational Series, Inc., Hauppauge, NY, 2005.

Lucanus, Oliver, and Gary Elson. *The Barb Aquarium.* Barron's Educational Series, Inc., Hauppauge, NY, 2005.

Mills, Dick. *Encyclopedia of Aquarium Fish.* Barron's Educational Series, Inc., Hauppauge, NY, 2000.

Ostrow, Marshal E. *Goldfish.* Barron's Educational Series, Inc., Hauppauge, NY, 2003.

Sandford, Gina. *The Tropical Aquarium.* Barron's Educational Series, Inc., Hauppauge, NY, 2004.

Schmida, Gunther. *Rainbowfish.* Barron's Educational Series, Inc., Hauppauge, NY, 2000.

Scott, Peter W. *The Complete Aquarium.* DK Publishing, Inc., New York, NY, 1995.

Smith, Mark Phillip. *Tetras and Other Characins.* Barron's Educational Series, Inc., Hauppauge, NY, 2005.

Stadelmann, Peter, and Lee Finley. *Tropical Fish.* Barron's Educational Series, Inc., Hauppauge, NY, 2003.

Zurlo, George, and David Schleser.*Cichlids.* Barron's Educational Series, Inc., Hauppauge, NY, 2005.

Magazines

Aquarium Fish Magazine
www.aquariumfish.com

Freshwater & Marine Aquarium
www.famamagazine.com

Tropical Fish Hobbyist
www.trh.com

Cover: Angelfish; back cover: male Siamese Fighting Fish at bubble nest (top), Flag Acara (center), Starlight Bristlenose Catfish (bottom).

The Photographers
Back to Nature Aquaristik GmbH; Bork; Büsher; Giel; Hartl; Hecker; Juniors/Peither; Kahl; Kölle; Linke; Lucas; Nieuwenhuizen; Peither; Schmida; Schmidbauer; Silvestris online/Lacz; Spreinat; Staeck; Untergasser; and Werner.

Acknowledgments
The author and publisher thank attorney Reinhard Hahn for legal advice, as well as the firm Back to Nature Aquaristik GmbH, Lauenau (*www.back-to-nature.de*) for providing photos of aquarium backgrounds.

© Copyright of English-language translation 2008
by Barron's Educational Series, Inc.

Original title of the book in German: *300 Fragen zum Aquarium*
© Copyright 2005 by Gräfe und Unzer Verlag GmbH, Munich, Germany

Translation from the German by Mary D. Lynch

All inquiries should be addressed to:
Barron's Educational Series, Inc.
250 Wireless Boulevard
Hauppauge, NY 11788
www.barronseduc.com

Library of Congress Control No.: 2006930970

ISBN-13: 978-0-7641-3715-0
ISBN-10: 0-7641-3715-8

Printed in China
9 8 7 6 5 4 3 2 1